ULTIMATE
COURSE **FORMULA**

——HOW TO——
CREATE AND SELL
YOUR ONLINE COURSE
IN 60 DAYS OR LESS

IMAN AGHAY

Spotlight PUBLISHING

Goodyear, AZ

Ultimate Course Formula: How to Create and Sell Your Online Course in 60 Days or Less by Iman Aghay, Creator of Ultimate Course Formula

Print Book ISBN: 978-1-7337388-3-5
eBook ISBN: 978-1-7337388-4-2

Published by Success Road Enterprises | Spotlight Publishing™

Table of Contents

Introduction

Welcome to the Ultimate Course Formula. Congratulation on the best decision you ever made when it come to building your online program. This book will open the door to some amazing opportunities for you in building your busines, building the foundation of your marketing, and using your knowledge to change other peoples lives.

This book is about to change the way you think and the way you perform in your business. It will show you how you can make a huge difference in your life and the lives of others by sharing your expertise. It will show you how to achieve financial freedom, location freedom, and time freedom. I'm super-excited for you.

Now, this is an important note: Make sure that you follow the steps that I've outlined in this book one step at a time. This is a system that has been tested by hundreds of people who have gotten amazing results.

It's not something that you'll want to change. I can tell you for a fact that any time a student tried to skip the steps, or change the steps, or reinvent the wheel, or not follow the process, it took them longer and made it much harder for them. They didn't get the results that they were hoping for, and they had to redo everything from scratch.

At times it may not be clear why certain things are done in a certain way, or a certain order, but as you go through the program, you'll realize every piece is building on top of a prior step.

If you skip a step, you will be missing a piece you will need in the future, and that's going to hurt you. By the end of this book, if you follow the steps and do all the exercises, you will be able to launch your beta user group, which will be your first group of students.

To be clear, when you are building an online course, the first thing you want to do is to make sure you have sold the course first. After you have sold the course, you teach the course to a beta group, your first students who will give you feedback on the course.

As you teach your first group, you will get competence and confidence. Then you can go and rerecord the course and create the recorded version of it.

You never, ever create the live version of the course without selling it first and never create the recorded version of the course without teaching it live, to a group of people who can give you feedback so you can improve it.

By the end of this book, you will be able to launch your beta group. I'm going to teach you how to attract those people, how to sell your course first, how to create your course and start teaching it.

You'll deliver the content to your beta students – a group of people or even one person, one session at a time. That allows you to put together your content easily, and as you start recording your content, you'll learn a lot about the technology.

You'll also have your membership area set up. When you record your course, those pieces of content need to be secured in one area, which is why you will need a membership area. Then you'll learn how to use your online course to increase your prices. That's probably the most important thing that you can do.

Having an online course increases the value of your time.

Here's why:

With an online course, you are providing value without you being personally involved. When you are providing value without being personally involved, that allows you to have more value when you are personally involved. As a result, you can increase the prices that you charge for direct group and individual coaching.

Now, let's talk about the eight steps of course creation. As I said, complete one step at a time and don't skip any. We start with your business model and understanding the fundamentals.

This is the first thing you want to do even before creating your course. Many times, people say they want to create a course, and the first question they ask is, "What's the course supposed to be about?" That's the wrong place to start.

The first question you need to ask is, "What's the best course for me to create to benefit my business? What's the course that I need today to help me to grow my business in the future?"

You have to start with your business model, and understand the fundamentals of online courses, understand how your online course can benefit you. That's Step 1.

After you decide why you want to create an online course, what type of customers you want to attract, and how your online course is going to fit into your bigger picture for marketing, then we go to Step 2.

Step 2 is creating an irresistible offer, testing your course concept, and discovering whether your offer is going to work or not.

There's a specific type of market research that you have in Step 2, and you're going to use that research to put together the structure of your content.

Module 1.1

The Business Model

The first step, when it comes to online course creation is understanding your business model. If you don't understand that foundation of online course creation, you're going to have a really hard time making online course work.

Your course is not the final goal. Building your business is. Sometimes people create an online course, they sell $10,000 or $50,000 worth of that online course, and then their sales stop, their passion dies, or their course doesn't work anymore. Then what?

When it comes to online courses, it's very important that you use the course as part of your bigger marketing strategy. I've never seen any online course creator who is a successful seven-figure earner from online course creation who has created only one course. We all create one course, and that course becomes the foundation of a second course and third course and fourth course.

I have more than 50 online courses, but I didn't create all of them together at the same time. Six years ago, when I created my first course, I didn't even know what my topic should be. So, you don't have to have your grand ideas right at the beginning, but keep in mind from the start that your online course should be part of your bigger marketing strategy. For that, I'm going to cover the benefits of online courses for your business.

At the foundational level, you need to understand that while you are providing information in your course, knowledge is not what makes the difference in people's lives. It's the accountability and the support that makes the biggest difference. Most of the time, I would say 95% of people who want to create online courses start by thinking about their knowledge. They say, "Iman, there are lots of YouTube videos out there. Why would people want to buy my course?" or "Why would people want to pay $2,000 for a course, when they can buy a $25 book?"

That's fair enough, but you need to understand that knowledge is not what changes people's lives. A person wanting to lose weight might know that they should eat less and exercise more.

But, does that help that person lose weight? No, because knowledge is not what changes people's lives. What changes people's lives is having accountability and support.

When it comes to creating an online course, there are lots of people who are only thinking about giving people knowledge. They are thinking, "Oh, I'm going to create the course, and I'm going to give people the knowledge. I'm going to give people the steps and the system. I'm going to give people ideas. And if they use those ideas and the systems, they can get results."

To a certain point that is true, but these types of online courses – we call them the foundational courses – are courses that give people lots of ideas. These are equivalent to reading books. You can do that, but most likely you are looking at charging $25, $50 or $100 for a course like that.

However, what creates better value is to add more accountability and support. The more that you add, the better the course and the more value you are going to create for your students.

"When I met Iman, I was down to my last reserves and was in a dire sink or swim situation. I attended one of his events and was immediately so inspired and confident I could succeed with his system if I decided to sign on. It was a huge decision to invest my remaining funds in Iman's program and tutelage, but on the other hand, I felt it was my only chance. I'm so very glad I did!

By following his system, my revenue has doubled every year, is now six figures, and I'm just getting started. Iman encourages me to set high goals and each year I discover I have achieved them. He is ingenious at designing simple win-win marketing solutions which benefit my clients as much as me.

I started Ultimate Course Formula and launched online training programs last autumn, and earned 27,000 of online sales in eight weeks without advertising or even sending emails through my list. I'm equal parts grateful and excited about this coming year, which is a great situation to find myself in. If you are serious about launching online programs with your business, I recommend you get started today!"

Arrow Gonsalves
Creator of Human Energetics

Module 1-2

CHAPTER 1 CONTINUED

Three Levels of Online Courses

When it comes to your business, there are three types of customers that you deal with as coaches, consultants, authors, and speakers.

Interested Customers

The first group is comprised of interested people. The interested group of people is people who always want to get knowledge. They want to go to free webinars, free seminars, and free evening events. They are the ones who want to pick your brain.

There are lots of interested people out there. Think about people who are interested in weight loss. They'll ask a weight-loss expert, "Can I ask you a question about my weight loss? Should I eat this food or not?"

They're always looking for free information, or maybe they're willing to invest a little money, such as $7 or $10, up to a maximum $97 or $100. They're willing to buy books and watch lots of free YouTube videos. They like doing all these types of things, but they are not heavily invested in getting results. They think if they get the knowledge, they're good to go.

As I said earlier, we know that knowledge alone will not get people results. What gets people results is support and accountability.

Qualified Customers

The second group of people is people who are done wasting their time asking for free advice or watching YouTube videos. They want to get a step-by-step system and support from a person who already knows how to get something done, and they're willing to pay to get results. These are qualified customers.

The qualified group of people are usually totally fine with investing $500 to $2,000 to get an organized system. They want to buy a course where somebody can take their hand, show them the way, give them feedback, and get them results. They're happy to be part of a community where the other members are also interested in getting results.

In some niche markets, that range of investment can change. In some cases, the qualified buyer might start at about $250, and in other cases, in heavier money-generating niche markets, a qualified buyer might be ready to spend $5,000 on a course. But, generally, we say that courses between $500 and $2,000 are qualified courses.

Committed Customers

The final group of customers is made up of those who are truly committed to their success. They want to invest heavily in themselves on getting the results they want. They want to work with someone one-on-one and get that person to take their hand and walk them every step of the way. They are emotionally invested, time invested and financially invested, and they want to get results.

A personalized program like that could be well over $5,000 and can go as high as $1 million depending on who is teaching it. There's no ceiling for those types of programs.

The question for you is what type of customer do you want in your business? Do you want an interested group of customers who want free advice? Do you want a qualified group of people willing to invest something on themselves by going into a group program to get support and results? Or do you want a committed group of hand-selected clients who are willing to invest in themselves heavily to get massive results? Which one are you more interested in? Which one do you need in your business?

I know that most likely, you're going to go with the committed group. You're saying, "Oh, I think that I need the committed group of people who are willing to pay thousands of dollars."

But the reality is that you need all three groups of customers. You will never be a world-class expert if you are not sharing your content and information with lots and lots of interested people. The interested group of customers is the group that makes you well-known. They are the ones who could become your champions and talk about you everywhere because they get your information.

The qualified group of people is a group of people who are getting your work and getting the results. You cannot attract qualified people if you don't have access to interested people because all qualified people were at some point in the interested group. They get your free content, and then they say, "Yes, I want to work with you! I want to pay you for it!"

Finally, you have the committed group, those in the higher-end programs. You're not going to get them to pay $75,000 just from interacting with them once, without knowing them at all. Most likely, most of the clients that are attracted to the highest level have worked with you from your free content and your lower- priced offerings.

As I said, none of us who are world-class experts or building successful companies have only one course. We have created several courses, but the reason that we've created several courses is that each of our courses is directed to one of these groups of people. We have several courses for interested people. We have several courses for qualified people. We have several courses for committed people. You never end up creating only one course, but you create one course at a time.

The question for you here is: What group of people do you need today?

I'm going to share a few examples with you, and then I'm going to talk about different types of clients and which ones you need at what point. For example, in my business, Ultimate Course Formula is one of my courses that is divided into three sections or levels. There is a book version of it, which provides the knowledge, there is a boot camp training, which is a series of recorded videos, and there is a mentorship level.

The book is about $25, which is a pretty standard price compared with other markets where books usually land in the $18-$30 range. The boot camp training is around $2,000. That's the group coaching that people study, submit their homework on the Facebook group, and can get feedback. At the mentorship level, they work with a mentor one-on-one for six months, and it's $8,000.

I want you to understand that the knowledge between all three in the Ultimate Course Formula is the same. However, do you think the results that the mentorship student gets is the same as the result of the person who reads the book? Absolutely not! The results are drastically different between people who just read the book or people who are working with a mentor who has created hundreds of online courses with others and is now taking their student's hand.

Sometimes students say to me, "Iman, I don't have a lot of knowledge to create lots of different courses." Many times, you don't have to. It can be one piece of knowledge, and that piece of knowledge gets divided with different levels of support and accountability, and you create different layers of products for it; the $25 level, $2,000 level, and 8 or 10 or 20 or $30,000 level based on the exact same knowledge. That's the first mindset shift that I want you to get. You don't always need new knowledge to create new packages.

Now, what if we want to create different packages based on different knowledge? We can put them in different levels. For example, Ultimate Course Formula is the foundational level for us. It's the first piece that any of our students start with. Ultimate Course Formula in the group coaching version is a $2,000 course.

However, when people study the Ultimate Course Formula, they will also need to learn about traffic, so they're going to learn about credibility. Then they need to learn about conversion, or how to run Facebook ads. They want to learn about sales psychology or learn how to sell from the stage, how to become better public speakers, or how to become a number 1 best selling author.

All those become the next level. That can include $5,000 courses like Traffic Mastery, Conversion Mastery, and Credibility Mastery. Many of the people who are at that level said, "You know what? I want to belong to a community of successful entrepreneurs so we can promote each other, help each other, and we can bounce ideas off of each other."

Some of them are doing six-figure events or want to do six-figure events, so they say, "You know what? I want to learn about all of this because I want to build a successful business, so I need to belong to a mastermind and mentorship program." Those individuals go to our higher-level LEAD Mastermind Program.

And then, some of those people at that level say, "You know what? I want to work one-on-one with Iman." That's the mentorship level. That's the highest level at which you can provide service to someone. For us, for example, my Rising Star Experts Mentorship Program, at the time that I'm writing this, is a $75,000 annual investment.

So you see, it can go all the way from a $25 program to a $75,000 program, but every piece is building on the other. Most of these courses are online. Ultimate Course Formula is an online course, Traffic Mastery, Conversion Mastery, they're all online courses that each have a three-day live event, and LEAD Mastermind is a combination of all of it.

It's 80% online, plus three 3-day live events. The Rising Star Experts mentorship program is technically LEAD Mastermind plus a one-on-one session with me every two weeks.

So, what I want you to understand is that you will create different levels. Maybe not today, maybe not tomorrow, but a year down the road, you are going to have a series of courses that build on top of each other. You can't just go and have a $75,000 program.

You can't go only for committed people. How would you market it? You have to have a funnel. You have to have a system where you attract interested people, and then that system separates the interested people from qualified people, and that system separates the qualified people from the committed people.

That's why I say you need different courses at different levels. The question here for you is, which one do you need today? If you're just getting started, you don't have any mailing list, nobody knows you, and you're starting absolutely from scratch, you'll probably need to provide free content. You need a course for interested people, so that way you can attract many people. That's how you can build the foundation.

If you've been in a market, and people know you, but you're not getting paid properly, and you don't have an automated stream of income, then you need a qualified course. You need a course between $500 and $2,000.

If you have been in the market, you are charging $500 to $2,000 easily and comfortably, but you want to get paid far better, or you're doing a lot of one-on-one sessions, you want to separate your time from your value, and you want to charge higher prices, then you need a course for the committed group of people.

Here is one suggestion that would apply to most people who are studying this course. I would suggest that you can create a course for qualified people offering one 45-minute to 90-minute webinar for the interested people.

Some people get confused between the webinar and an online course.

A webinar is just one piece of content where, at the end of it, you sell something, such as your course. The webinar can be used to attract many attendees and help build your list of interested people to whom you will sell your course.

Now, don't get overwhelmed or scared, thinking, "Oh my God, how am I going to get people on the webinar? How am I going to do this?" You're not there yet, so don't worry about it. Don't start solving problems that you don't have yet. Ultimate Course Formula is going to walk you every step of the way.

We're going to teach you one step at a time, and we're going to share with you exactly how you can build your webinar, how to put together your system.

> **You don't always need new knowledge to create new packages.**

 ᭬

"I bought a course creation program a few years ago and still never completed it, but Ultimate Course Formula put me into action right away to get me real results and achieve completion!

What I needed was accountability to show up and do the work, which is exactly what UCF gave me. Because of taking UCF, I now have a group program which generated income for me right away. As soon as I launched my first beta course just a couple of months ago, it added over SK to my bottom line. I started with three students, which quickly grew to seven!

It's amazing! If I did my course the way I was planning on doing it, my course would not have the value to my customers that it has today. Sometimes you think you know what your customers need, but this totally changed after doing the market research module of the UCF course. The market research was so valuable, and I will use it over and over again. Also, being able to go live online to ask questions was so helpful because it got me past my roadblocks.

Action brings results. So, if you want to have results in your business, then you need to take action, and if you sign up for this course, it will give you everything you need so it cannot fail. If you follow all the steps in the course, it will bring you results!"

Jocelyne Devisser
Founder of JJ Cost Keeping, Inc.

Module 1-3

CHAPTER 1 (CONT'D)

8 Ways to Benefit from Online Courses

Another piece you need to know about online courses is how you can benefit from online courses in your business. The reason you need to understand this is because it will help you build a better online course.

As I said, many people build the wrong online course, and that will hurt them in the future. One of the top reasons for building the wrong online courses is because people don't know how to benefit from them.

Here are eight ways to benefit from online courses:

Increasing Prices

If you're a coach or consultant right now, you're teaching people something over and over. You can take that material and record an online course based on it. Your recording can be a 20-minute piece, a 30-minutes piece, or a 50-minute piece, but now that piece can become part of your packages.

When you're working with people one-on-one, instead of spending your time teaching the same thing over and over, you give people that piece of video. Tell them, "You know what? I'm not going to spend my time one-on-one with you to teach you this piece. You can study this piece of recording, and it teaches you everything.

After you study the recording, then get your homework done. Come back to me, and we'll customize it for you in your one-on-one session. That way, instead of spending our time to teach you the basic knowledge, we will be able to work on more advanced implementable materials."

Can you see how much you increase the value of what you're offering? When you increase the value of what you're offering, you can increase your prices. That's how you use an online course to increase your prices.

Automated Income

The second benefit of an online course is automated income because, once your online courses are created, they can be uploaded to a membership site and sold automatically.

Improving Customer Satisfaction

Imagine you are doing something in your business and your customers are not 100% sure or clear about how to use your services. You can create courses specifically on how to benefit more from the services that you're offering.

For example, if you're a web designer and you want your customers to have higher customer satisfaction, and you're building WordPress websites for them, you can easily put together some courses on how they can manage their WordPress websites after they bought their site from you.

You've helped increase your customer satisfaction because now the customer can go and review all those training videos and get the benefit from them. They will value your web design services because you helped them manage their website more effectively.

List Building

By creating free courses, you can build your mailing list. A course can be a simple PDF, it can be recorded videos, or it can be a webinar. They will all allow you to build your list.

Sometimes, people who are just getting started come to me and tell me, "Iman, I don't have a mailing list, so I can't create a course." I say, "No, that's the other way around. You can't build a list if you don't have a course." You always start by building your course, and by using your course, you build your mailing list.

Rejuvenating an Existing List

You can use your online course to find other people who have large lists and haven't been using them.

Why would someone have a "dead" mailing list? Have you ever done something in your life that you lost passion for? Let's say five or six years ago you were doing something and you were very excited about it and then you lost your passion for it.

For example, lots of experts started with online marketing. They built a large list for themselves in any niche market – in stress management, in finances, in marketing, in whatever. They did it for four, five, six years, and they have 50,000, 100,000, 200,000 people on their list. Now, they don't have any passion for running it anymore, or they don't have the products or the services to serve the list.

That's a great opportunity for you. You can use your course to rejuvenate that person's list. You start by teaching those people something for free, building your own list from the stale list, build your group of interested people, create courses for qualified people, and then go to the next level. There are lots of lists out there. The biggest one that I dealt with was a 250,000-person mailing list that someone had built years ago. They didn't know how to rejuvenate it and had lost the passion for taking care of it.

There are so many of these lists out there, but sometimes people say to me, "Yes, Iman, you have access to those type of lists, but we don't." The reality is, when you're out networking, there's a very high chance that you have talked to many of those people who have those lists, but they never told you because you didn't have the foundation to benefit from it, or you never asked.

Sales Funnel

You can use your online course to build your sales funnel. Start with a free online course, and then you create a tripwire offer. A tripwire offer is a low-cost product, like a $7 to $20 course that an interested person might buy. It's a small investment, and they get to work with you, and hopefully love what you are teaching. After that, you offer them a $497 course. That starts your sales funnel.

Expanding Reach While Decreasing Costs

Back in 2013 and 2014, we used to do about 200 live events a year in four cities. I used to travel from one city to the next. We had two offices in downtown Vancouver. I had hundreds of students who had to come to a local office, to a local place for us to be able to serve them. When we went online, I stopped traveling to deliver my content and gave up my offices.

I travel because I enjoy traveling around the world. We have clients around the globe, in Australia, the U.K., Germany, and in Switzerland; however, I don't need to travel to teach anymore, so online courses have decreased our travel costs.

We don't need to have offices anymore. The whole business is online. We have far more students than we had back in 2014. Our costs have decreased drastically because everything is online.

If you have a lot of costs related to your office, travel or venues for live training, seriously look into seeing what part of your business you can take online so you can save money.

Expanding Your Experts Network

When I talk about your expert's network, I'm referring to both the trainers and the promoters who support your training. Let's say, for example; you have a person that really likes you, has a mailing list of 50,000 people and wants to promote you. If you don't have an online course, that person can't promote you, because you cannot handle 50,000 people wanting to work with you one-on-one. When you create an online course, you're expanding your reach because you will have access to a network of promoters who can promote you effectively.

Also, you can expand your circle of trainers. There may be so much you want to teach, and you don't have the specific knowledge. If you are online and you want someone else to teach that material to your students, you can simply connect online with any trainer anywhere in the world to come and teach your classes for you as long as they have Internet access.

"I've been creating and teaching online courses for years. However, like in anything you do, there are gaps in your knowledge, and new technologies and services are always becoming available. Iman's Ultimate Course Formula filled those knowledge gaps and prepared me to MUCH better select courses that sell more easily while serving my students better. I have made some critical changes to my marketing strategy and my course structures.

My confidence is now substantially higher, knowing I have all the pieces rather than just most of the pieces to offer successful online courses. The resources Iman shares, his breadth of knowledge, and the completeness of his UCF makes it an easy, easy investment to justify."

Michael Angier
Founder and Inspiration Officer atSuccessNet.org

CHAPTER 1 (CONTINUED)

Three Types of Experts

Many times when we are creating an online course, we ask ourselves what type of expert we are. When people are creating an online course, they often question their expertise because they haven't achieved massive success in business or in life in the things they want to teach.

Have you ever wondered, "Can I create an online course if I haven't achieved massive success in those areas?" The answer to that is, "Absolutely yes!"

This experience is often called "imposter syndrome." Many experts doubt themselves because they don't know there are three types of experts. If you understand what type of expert you are and have made an honest assessment of where you are, you start from there and grow over time. You will get better and build more success around you and become a role model over time.

Here are the three types of experts:

- Results Expert
- Role Model Expert
- Interviewer Expert

You might be one or two or even all three.

The Results Expert

The results experts are the experts who have expertise and knowledge in a certain area. They can help others achieve a certain result. Sometimes those experts haven't necessarily achieved those results, or aren't necessarily the best, but they are good at teaching how to do it.

For example, when you watch a football game, you look at the coach of the game, and think, "this guy couldn't kick the ball himself!" That football coach doesn't have to be the best football player to be able to coach football. Some of the coaches who run the top-level teams have never played the game as a pro, but they can see the plays and know how to bring out the best in the players.

It's the same when it comes to other areas in life. For example, there are university professors who teach marketing at the best universities in the world who are not necessarily the best marketers in the world, but they are training some of the best marketers in the world. To teach something, you don't necessarily have to be able to do it.

There are other things that you may be good at, either teaching or doing for others, but you're not good at doing them for yourself. Some of those abilities are what we call your gifts.

Every person is born with 24 gifts. Some of those gifts are dormant; some of those gifts are active. When you have a gift in you, when things are gifted to you, technically you are very good at doing it for others, but that does not mean that you're doing it for yourself. That's the definition of a gift.

I'm sure that you've heard of many people who are really good managers of another person's company, but they can't be really good entrepreneurs in their own business. I'm sure that you have seen people who are good at going to another person's home or office and organizing everything for them, but when it comes to their own space, it's always a mess.

If you're good at teaching something to someone, you're good at it. Don't question yourself. Don't doubt yourself. You don't necessarily have to be the greatest implementer to be the greatest teacher for that particular material. People can use your services and benefit from what you teach, and you can make a massive difference in their lives.

The Role Model Expert

Role model experts are people who have done something for themselves, they have created a system for doing it the way that they do it, and they can teach people exactly how they've achieved certain types of success following that specific system. They have done something to achieve massive success, now they're putting it into a system, and they're teaching it to others.

For example, when it comes to online course creation, I'm a role model expert. I've created 50 online courses. I have a specific step-by-step system that I've tested over and over. I've generated a great deal of money while creating and selling my online courses. Now I can teach my students how to follow the same step-by-step process that I use when it comes to online course creation. That makes me a role model expert.

Most role model experts started from being a results expert. Generally, role model experts are paid more than the results experts because they have achieved a certain level of success.

The Interviewer Expert

Interviewer experts are the people who interview other experts in a niche market. You don't need to have all the content or all the knowledge yourself. For example, in my LEAD Mastermind Program, we have courses in which we are teaching about Facebook ads and Facebook groups.

Now, I'm not a world-class expert when it comes to Facebook ads. I'm not a world-class expert when it comes to Facebook groups. What I've done is that I've found these experts who are the best in these areas and interviewed them about their expertise. Sometimes we even hire them to teach our students directly. Sometimes they contribute their content in exchange for other content that I've created.

As part of the Ultimate Course Formula, you will see lots of these shorter interviews that I've done 20-minute, 30-minute, 50-minute videos. For example, how to sell your online course to a corporation. I can teach my students how to sell to corporations without even having sold anything to corporations, not because of my knowledge, but because I use another person's knowledge. I interview that person and share that person's expertise.

Sometimes we need to pay these experts and sometimes not. Most of the time you don't need to pay them, especially if you're presenting them as part of a qualified course. You are featuring them in your program and giving them exposure, which is what they want.

Today, in this day and age, the most important thing everybody wants is exposure. If I'm putting these experts in front of my students, they're getting exposure to my students, so they're happy to share their content and get exposure in return.

Many times, you start as one type of expert, and you evolve in your career. Back in 2011, when I started my journey, I knew that I wanted to create courses, but I didn't know what course I wanted to create. I knew that I wanted to create a course for entrepreneurs. I knew I was good at marketing, but I didn't know what type of marketing I wanted to do. I didn't know what type of course I wanted to teach – what would resonate with students. I was telling people I teach online marketing, and everybody would ask me what I meant because it was too broad.

At the time, I didn't have a large company. When I started, I was 17 days away from becoming homeless. That's when I started my first company. I was nobody. I had no content, no nothing. I gathered eight people, and I said, "I want to share with you for eight weeks how to do online marketing."

The first thing I did was ask them what they wanted to learn about online marketing. They gave me a list of everything they wanted to learn, and I put it on a wall. There were so many different things – how to market events, how to become a best-selling author, how to create an online course, how to build a YouTube channel, how to become a celebrity on Facebook or Twitter, or how to manage your social media.

I chose one topic, and I started teaching that one piece. I developed my content over the next eight weeks. Now, mind you, at that time, I wasn't an expert. I wasn't a world-class leader. I wasn't even running a six-figure business. I hadn't done any large events myself. However, I had the knowledge. I knew how to teach it.

As a result of the first group of classes that I ran, one of my students went from running a 12-person event to a 540-person event in 45 days. He had been putting on events for 12 years, and the biggest event he could put together was 12 people. Now, at the time, I hadn't done a 540-person event myself, but that didn't stop me from teaching this person how to do a 540-person event.

I had another student in the class who was trying to get contracts with corporations. At the time, I didn't have any contracts with corporations myself, but using the model that I taught, he went out, and he got solidly booked for the next six months. Moreover, he did that within the 45 days that I taught the course.

Although I hadn't achieved any of those results, I had students who were doing large events and were solidly booked as public speakers, who were doing lots of other things in their careers.

Those became examples of my success stories. When I did my next event, I brought the success stories of these students and talked about the amazing results they got from taking my course. Then, more people went to the back of the room and started signing up for my program. As a result of that, I built a six-figure company in the coaching world.

So, I started as a results expert, and that helped me to create success. That success made me a role model expert. Then when I took my company to seven figures, that made me a bigger role model expert. I was a world-class expert teaching people how to build seven-figure companies, and creating and selling online courses. That didn't start with me knowing what I was doing or having any examples to follow. So you see, in the beginning, I was also questioning myself.

One thing that's very important for you to know is that if you want to become a coach and you want to do this successfully, you must commit to one thing and that one thing is serving your customers with excellence. With the first group of eight people that I taught, I went above and beyond to make sure that they became successful. I provided everything they needed, above and beyond the package that I sold them, to make sure that they could get results.

The first time I taught Ultimate Course Formula, I made sure every single one of my students achieved massive success. From serving them with excellence, I learned what pieces I needed to add to the package so my students could achieve success. You learn how to create better packages by teaching. Then when you serve your students with excellence, and they get results, they become your success stories, your testimonials, and your case studies.

I have over a thousand students who have created successful courses. They're doing events, seminars, conferences, public speaking, and consulting work, all because one day, I started as a role model expert.

If at some point in your training, you learn that you lack a piece of content, there is no downside to interviewing people and becoming an interviewer expert.

Whatever market you're going after, you can easily find the content through interviewing people. You can become a results expert, or you can be a role model expert. Put the imposter syndrome aside, serve people with excellence, and you can make a big difference in other people's lives, and also have massive success in your own business.

> *If you want to become a coach and you want to do this successfully, you must commit to one thing, and that one thing is serving your customers with excellence.*

"Iman Biock Aghay totally rocks! I think these trainings are brilliant! Simple, effective, succinct, and crystal clear -you just can't beat it!"

Dr. Irena Kay
Founder of The Relationship Success Equation

Module 1-5

CHAPTER 1 (CONTINUED)

The Harmonized Business Model

When it comes to building your online course, you need to make sure that it is part of your harmonized business model.

A harmonized business model is the system where you target one group or niche market, you give them one solution, and you serve those people with that solution to higher and higher levels. It's a system that allows you to make your marketing ten times easier.

For example, if you create an online course for lawyers, the first group of students that you will attract to the course will all be lawyers. Then, if the second course that you have will be for the lawyers who studied the first course, you don't need that much effort to market the second course. Why? Because you have a big group of lawyers who are going through the first of your courses and they're going to be interested in getting the second course.

So, instead of trying to market your courses to new groups of people, you market to one group of people, and that one group will trickle down to every next step that you have.

For example, in my business, Ultimate Course Formula is for coaches, consultants, authors, and speakers, whom we refer to as experts who want to make a difference. So, it's for people who are sharing their knowledge and expertise and are making money by selling their content.

Once these knowledge bringers create and sell their online courses, then they say, "Now, I need to learn how to do webinars." So, the next course we have is on webinars. Then they say, "I need to do my Facebook ads" or "I need to become a public speaker" or "I need to become a world-class leader." Every course that we have is for the same group of knowledge bringers. That's how you choose one group of people, so you don't need to reinvent the wheel and do the scattered marketing.

Remember, getting to any niche market is expensive. So instead of trying to get into a new niche market for every single course that you create, you create one course, and then you go deeper and deeper with that niche market.

Another thing you need to understand is that there are a million ways to generate a million dollars. You can make one sale at $1 million. You can make two sales of half-a-million dollars each. You can make three sales of $333,333. You can even sell one million things at $1. There are a million ways to make a million dollars.

Sometimes people will ask me, "Iman, what's the best way to generate money online?" Should we create a $2,000 course or a $1,000 course? What's the best niche market to follow? What's the best topic to follow?"

Two key points I always emphasize are:

Make sure your niche and topic are really aligned, and your topic should be a million-dollar idea.

What does a million-dollar idea look like? A million-dollar idea is an idea that provides you with a new way within the million ways to generate the million dollars.

For example, if you can find 1,000 people who pay you $1,000 each for that topic, then it's a million-dollar idea. If you can find 2,000 people who will pay you $500 each, that's still a million-dollar idea. If you create a course that's $100,000 and can find ten people who each pay you $100,000, that's still a million-dollar idea.

What you want to do any time you are planning your course is to put it through a million-dollar idea test. You want to say, "Can I find any combination with which I can generate a million dollars from this course?"

That doesn't mean that you will generate a million dollars from this course. However, it shows you that there is the potential to generate the million dollars.

If there is not, then most likely it isn't a good niche market to start with. For example, a few years back, I had a student who wanted to create a course for a specific type of custom guitar builders. He wanted to teach them certain things and how to do a certain type of work. The course he wanted to create was not an expensive course. He was thinking about selling it for about $50.

When he went out and started finding potential clients, he found fewer than 50 guitar builders interested in the types of things he could teach them. Even before creating the course, you know that course is destined to fail. You should not create that course because that's not a million-dollar idea.

I had another student who was building a course on confidence. The type of course that he wanted to build he could easily sell for $200. It was very easy to find 5,000 people to pay $200 for that course. So there we have it. It's a million-dollar idea. It's a good course to build. It doesn't matter how much the price of the course is if you can find enough people. However, if the course is really low-priced and you can't find enough people to buy it, you can't turn it into a million-dollar idea.

Different Income Models

Now let's look at our online courses in a harmonized business model and see how we can make that work. When it comes to an online course, there are different income models that you can follow. You can create one online course that is a paid course and, as a result of that paid course, people learn something from you and then go to another paid course.

The next type of model you can use is that of an independent course – one course on its own that's not going to lead to another course. However, as part of that independent course, you invite people to get a one-hour one-on-one consultation session with you. When you do the one-on-one consultation, you invite them to buy a service or a product.

Let's say, for example, you are a graphic designer or a web designer, and you can have an independent course called, "How to build a killer website" or "How to have a website that converts many clients for you."

The course may be a $500 course, but as part of it, students get a one-hour consultation session with you. You talk to them about their business, about their model, about everything. Then you say, "You know what? If you want, we can build your website for you. It's going to be only $5,000. If not, you can continue to follow the course." That person says, "You know what? If you credit that $500 of the online course to that $5,000, I'm more than happy to do this." So now you're selling your product or service by using an online course.

Another model you can use is one where you do a free training followed by a consultation session followed by a product or service. One of the things that my company is doing on Facebook, for example, is that we have a free webinar online. At the end of that free webinar, we invite people to a consultation session about their online courses that they want to build. They fill in the application form. They get on the phone with us. While we are on the phone with them, we invite them into our mentorship program, which is $8,000.

That's how we use the online course. It's a free training. It's just a free, small piece at the beginning that leads to a consultation session that leads to the sale of a product or service.

Now the last type of model, which is the model that I really like, starts with free training. You provide free training and then that free training leads into a series of inexpensive trainings.

Alternatively, you simply go from free training into one qualified course. That qualified course can lead to an event or a consultation session. From there, it leads to a high-ticket item.

A high-ticket item can be a $10,000 or $20,000 item. That is the model we use in our business. We do a free webinar, and we have lots of other free training online. From the free training, people can invest in Ultimate Course Formula or other programs that we have.

From there, they come to an event. At the event, they apply for our mastermind program, which is $25,000, or they choose our higher- level mentorship, which is $75,000. We use the online course technique as a funnel, and those who go through the funnel are the same clients who would go through our mastermind program as well.

We only promote one course at the top of the funnel. Often people who start there become our highest paying clients at the end, which makes a massive difference in your business and the way you run your company.

Always keep that in mind – when you want to build your business, you want to build a harmonized business model that leads people from one piece to the next piece to the next piece, so you don't end up creating online courses that you need to market every single time.

For example, say you have five online courses. You don't want to market all five online courses because it's very expensive and it's very time-consuming. You want to market one of the courses. That course will trickle down to everything else.

Homework

As your first homework assignment, build a Harmonized Business Model for yourself. It isn't going to be written in stone; you will probably change it. However, it will give you a great idea of where to get started. Try to figure out the best model, the best system you can create to generate income.

Below are a couple of examples of harmonized business models and the way that you'll need to do the homework.

For a Harmonized Business Model, you want to start by choosing a niche market. For the first example, the niche market is aspiring authors. The program the person is thinking of creating is publishing a book.

The Harmonized Business Model for this one would be a free e-book. You're going to give an interested person a free e-book that has templates to write and publish a book. That leads into a free video series. At the end of that free video series, you lead people to a paid course that's $1,497, which can be a book-writing mastermind group plus some online videos, plus some one-on-one support. When people are at that level in the mastermind, you invite them to use other paid services.

For the second example of a Harmonized Business Model, let's choose the niche market of overweight men, and the program is weight loss. In this model, you can start by speaking at conferences for men. That's how you start attracting people for free. Then you invite them to a free consultation talking one-on-one.

Then you can invite them to a monthly weight-loss program for $450 a month. For people who are in that level, if they want to work with you one-on-one, they can do an intense weight loss program, $1,500, six weeks, with one-on-one training twice per week.

Always remember that you want the first product, whatever that is, to lead to the second product, the third product, fourth product, and so on.

So now, create a similar Harmonized Business Model for yourself. Write a niche market. Write the program name. Then determine how you are going to use your online courses to attract people at different levels and different price points.

> **Make sure that your niche market
> and the topic is aligned with your
> passion, purpose, and skills.**

"OMG! I just woke up with the most amazing AH-HA in my business' mission, plan, message, and program! If there was anything I was uncertain about, it is now so very clear to me, and everything is now connected! I am SO GLAD that I listened to Iman.

Wow, did I ever get some mighty fabulous gems! Iman is truly the Changemaker's Mentor, and I've discovered how that is so immensely foundational to the path of my business. This business- transforming "lightbulb" moment is going to change EVERYTHING for me."

Venus Ramos MD
CEO & Founder of Dr. Venus

CHAPTER 2

Module 2-1

Technicality Versus Result: How to Find the Sweet Spot

In this chapter, we're going to look at something that has changed the lives of hundreds of our students because it has given them that secret sauce on how to create something that people want to buy. The secret is the ability to explain to the customer exactly what they want in their language! Have you ever wanted to sell something, and you said, "I wish I could explain it better?"

Do you wish you knew how to get people to tell you the words that they want to hear when they are buying the product so you can create an irresistible offer for them? In this section, I will explain how you get their language.

The very first step to do that is to distinguish between the technicality of what you're doing and the result of what you offer. As course creators, as content creators, we care a lot about the process. We care a lot about the system. We care a lot about the procedures that help people achieve certain results. We care about that more than the results. Why?

Because those are the things that we have to teach. When we're too close to our own content, we can't explain to people exactly what it is that they are buying, or what it is that they get from this. We want to talk more about what they'll do and how they'll do it, not what they'll get. We are so comfortable with the technicality that sometimes we forget that people don't know the details.

For example, sometimes people may ask me, "Iman, what's the best tool to use?" I can say, "Right now, the best tools for online trainers are a Logitech C920, a Yeti Blue, Caprice software, and Active Campaign." To me, that sounds very normal, but I sometimes forget that these are technical words that people may not understand.

It is the same thing when you're teaching anything, whether you're teaching finances, health, business, or marketing because you are an expert in it and you are too close to the content.

Because you are too comfortable with it, you talk about the technicalities instead of talking about the results, and that creates confusion for people. They can't understand what you're saying; they can't understand what you're doing.

A confused mind never makes a decision. When you talk about technicalities, and it confuses people, they can't make a decision, they can't move forward, and they're not going to take action. To be able to explain to people exactly what it is that you do, you need to find a sweet spot that people understand. If you are talking about something that is too technical, always ask yourself a question like, "What's the result of that?"

On the other hand, some people – around 20% of people – do the opposite. When you ask them a question, they talk about all the results and the dream and everything else, instead of saying anything about the technicality. This often ends up sounding like a scheme that's just too good to be true. Remember, the sweet part is somewhere between talking about the technicalities and talking about the results.

Let's take, for example, *Ultimate Course Formula*. Technically, what I'm teaching, you can be used for selling events, selling products, selling online courses, or even for becoming a public speaker. It is the foundation of the marketing that I'm teaching.

However, if I say, "Come and take a course on the foundation of the marketing," nobody is going to get it. Nobody is going to buy it because it's not specific, it's not giving me any specific results. When I make it specific about course creation, now you have a course creation course that people can understand.

As another example, let's say you want to teach people confidence. You tell them you are creating a course on confidence. Gaining confidence is the technicality of what you do, but if you focus on one niche market, let's say, for example, gaining confidence for parents, that course is far more interesting to people if they are parents.

A generic course on confidence that can help everyone is just too generic for people, and people don't get it; they don't understand it. They'll say, "Why would I get a course on confidence? I don't have confidence, but I don't see the value."

However, when you match it with a niche market, then say, "Okay, I want to teach you confidence, how to have confidence for your children," that's a fantastic course. Alternatively, how to be a confident public speaker. So it's not the technicality that matters that much; it's that niche market combined with the technicality that matters a lot.

With my courses, when people ask me what I teach, I can tell people I teach them how to write their Harmonized Business Model, how to do a specific type of market research, how to put together their content structure, and how to record their pieces of content. However, those are all the technicalities of what I do.

What I want to do is respond more about the results, so I'm going to ask myself, "What's the result of being able to do the market research? What's the specific result of being able to do the content structure?" Well, the specific result of it is that you can create a course that makes a difference in people's lives.

Okay, so what's the result of that? The result of that is that you can create a bigger academy, you can build a successful company. Okay, so what's the result of that? Well, the result of that is that you'll be able to build a company that makes an impact in the world, and because it's online, it gives you time, location freedom and financial freedom. Okay, great, so what's the result of that? Well, then you can live the life of your dreams. Having location freedom, time, freedom, and financial freedom, you can travel the world and enjoy the rest of your life.

Now you see how I went from the technicality – what it is that I do (I teach people how to do market research) all the way to, "You will be able to live your life free and enjoy your life, travel the world and do whatever you want." However, if someone asks me, "Iman, what do you teach?" and I say, "I teach people how to travel the world and enjoy their life, to have financial freedom, location freedom, and time freedom," that's sounds too good to be true, right? That sounds like a scam, and people might think, "Oh my God, what are you talking about?" That means you're emphasizing the result too much.

In the middle of that, there was one sweet spot, which was, "I help people to create and sell online courses in 60 days or less." That's not too dreamy and not too technical. It's the sweet spot.

It's the spot that people understand and can connect with. That needs to be the same in your market. You've got to ask yourself if what you're saying is the technicality of what you do, or is it the result. Then ask yourself, what's the result of that and what's the result of that and what's the result of that?

Sometimes I ask people what they do, and they might say, for example, especially if they are in health or holistic health, "I help people get into integrity with their body, mind, and soul." In the health world, that's too dreamy, that's too much toward the result. They have to go back toward the sweet spot, which means getting back to the technicality a little bit with this.

That might sound like, "I help people understand their truth and their values. I help people with understanding the type of food that they want and help them overcome the diseases that they have."

Okay, how do you do that? "Well, I do that through a test. I help them understand the mind. Alternatively, let's say 80% of people have leaky gut, I help them get better health in their gut and in their self."

Then when I ask how do you do that, they go to somewhere that's too technical that they can't even explain the purpose of the training.

However, there was a sweet spot there. The sweet spot is, "I help people who have digestion issues to learn about food and heal their digestive system, which then allows them to heal their body, that allows them to heal their body, mind, and soul,..." and so on.

The sweet spot, in this case, was to move closer toward the technicality than to the result. When you are too much toward the result, people don't get you, and when you are too much toward the technicality, people don't understand you. So this is one of the exercises for you. You want to go from the technicality toward the result and from the result toward the technicality and find that sweet spot for yourself. You've got to work on this until you get it right.

Remember, if you're too much in the technicality, ask yourself, "What's the result?" Then go to the next, next, next, next. If you are too much toward the result, you want to answer the question, "How do you do that?" Get to some of the technicalities so you can find that sweet spot.

One thing to keep in mind is that both your topic and your niche market should be very succinct – keep them each to about two to three words. You'll see why later in the book.

> **A confused mind never makes
> a decision.**

"I am so thankful for Iman's amazing and simple strategies and all of the reminders. It is easy to get thrown into the daily demands of life and family and forget what we need to do to continue the transformation. Iman helps with the importance of creating some of those success habits to help us become whom we want to be."

Dolores Storness-Bliss
Founder of Nature's Garden Real Food

CHAPTER 2 (CONTINUED)

Iman's 8 Golden Questions

Now that you know your topic and you know the niche market, it's time to go out and find eight to 20 people in your exact target market and ask them Iman's 8 Golden Questions.

This is probably the most important exercise you have for this entire course creation system, so it's very important that you do this correctly. I'm going to teach you how to find those eight to 20 people to interview, so don't worry about that right now. You'll get a specific message you can post on your Facebook and LinkedIn groups or email to friends and colleagues to ask people to meet with you.

For now, let's look at the eight questions. The key thing is that you don't want to change these questions. You don't want to add any words; you don't want to remove anything, you don't want to adjust it, so it feels good to you. If you do this part wrong, you have to redo everything from scratch. Stick to the exact thing that I'm going to share with you here; it's very important.

By the way, you're not going to do this online. You have to get on the phone with people. You don't want to send an email to people with the questions, and you don't want people to fill in a form. You want to get on the phone with people and have a two-way conversation with them. When you get on the phone, you just say, "Hey, thank you very much for accepting to do this interview with me. I really appreciate it; now let's begin." Then you begin with these questions.

Question 1:

When it comes to [the topic], what are the biggest challenges you are facing? Whatever your topic is, you're going to place it within those square brackets. As an example, online course creation is my topic, so I would ask, "When it comes to online course creation, what are your biggest challenges?" You're going to wait for them to answer you.

They might say, "My biggest challenge is not knowing what technology I should use." Then you would say, "Okay great. What else do you have a challenge with?" "Oh, my other challenge is not knowing how to put together my concept." "Great, so what other challenges you have?" You keep asking; you go deeper and deeper, "What else? What else?" It's very important to keep asking them what else there is.

Question 2:

When it comes to [the topic], what are the biggest fears you are facing? For this and every question, whatever they say, you write down exactly the way they said it.

It is very important that you write their words exactly the way that they say those words. Don't use other words or shorten their words or paraphrase. Write their sentences exactly the way that they are saying those sentences.

Why? Because you'll want to use those words, you'll want to use those sentences in your marketing in the future. If you change the words here, then your marketing isn't going to be aligned with what the customers want.

Question 3:

When it comes to [the topic], what are the biggest frustrations you are facing?

Sometimes they might ask you, "What's the difference between a challenge and a fear?" Or "How is a challenge different from my fears or frustrations?" The way that you would explain this is that, when you are challenged with something, you've tried to do it but you haven't been able to, or you haven't taken action because you're too overwhelmed or confronted to do it.

With fear, it usually comes with "I'm afraid of," so the sentences start with, "I'm afraid of." For example, a fear regarding online course creation is, "I'm afraid of creating my course, and nobody will want to buy it from me." That's a fear of online course creation. Or, "I'm afraid if I create the course that people won't like me on camera."

With frustration, the sentence starts with, "I'm frustrated." For example, "I'm frustrated by trying to get the technology to work." Frustrations are challenges that you keep trying to do, but you don't get results, so that turns into frustration.

What if you ended up putting a challenge on the fear list, or a fear on the frustration list? It doesn't matter. The first three answers are the pains that people are feeling, so at the end of the day, as long as the challenges, fears, and frustrations have been recorded, they're good to go.

We can still use these statements in marketing, and it wouldn't make any difference. Just remember to make sure to write their words exactly the way they said them. That's what matters.

Question No. 4:

What do you want to learn about [the topic]?

This is a very important question. Many people try to figure out what it is that they want to teach on their own and spend two or three months or more without knowing if it is the right content. The reality is that if you ask people what it is they want to learn, it just changes your life because they tell you exactly what it is they want to learn.

Now, having said that, what they want to learn is not necessarily what they need to learn. For example, when you decided to learn the Ultimate Course Formula, you wanted to learn how to create a course that sells incredibly well. You didn't know that you needed to learn Iman's 8 Golden Questions.

I know that you need to learn this, but you don't know. However, I still have to ask you what it is that you want to learn so that I can teach you what you need to learn. You're going to ask people in your target market what they want to learn.

Some pieces of what they want to learn may align with what they need to learn; some pieces may not, and you have to create other pieces to make it work, which is completely fine.

Question No. 5:

If you could get results from the things I'm going to teach you in this course, what would your dream day look like?

The key to this is that frequently people take courses not because they want to take the course, but because they want to get the results of that course.

For example, I know my target market for this course wants to create online courses. What they want is financial freedom, location freedom, and time freedom. They don't care about online course creation. They want to travel the world, do public speaking, and share their knowledge with the world – that's what they care about. The way to freedom is by learning how to create and sell online courses.

As the creator of the course, I need to understand that because, when I'm marketing my course, I've got to show people that what they really want are the benefits.

As a result of your online course, you can travel the world, enjoy your life, and make a difference in the world. For me, I need to understand what the real dreams of my clients are, so I can market my course and tell them how my course is going to help them to achieve those dreams.

That applies to every possible topic. Let's look at people who want to lose weight. Many people who want to lose weight want to run with their kids, they want to have more fun, they want to attract better mates, and so forth, but the goal isn't necessarily losing weight.

Most people who are overweight are not unhappy with being over-weight, but they are unhappy with the things that being overweight stops them from doing.

You need to understand the motivation behind your students and why they would take your course because that can help you when you are marketing it later on. You must ask them what a dream day looks like, and you want to write down exactly what they say.

Question No. 6:

What would you like to see in a package that makes you feel sup-ported enough to get results?

This question is the question that makes the biggest difference in your packages. As I said before, knowledge isn't what changes peo-ple's lives; it's knowledge, support, and accountability that changes people's lives.

When you ask this question, ask, "I want to create a package for you on [the topic] (online course creation, confidence, faith, weight loss, finances). What would you like to see in that package that would make you feel supported in helping you achieve the best results?"

This is a very important question, and most of the time they're not going to have an answer for you right away. However, it's very important that you stick to the question, and you can offer some more sugges-tions one at a time: If I want to create a package for you, what would you like me to put in the package?

- How many group coaching sessions?
- How many individual coaching sessions?
- How many videos?
- What do you want the videos to be about?
- What type of templates do you want?"
- What about a live event?
- More than one live event?

You want to get all those things answered before you move on to the next question. You are grilling them when you get to this question, but that makes a huge difference for you later on when you put together your package.

At the end, review what they said and then ask one more time: "What else do I need to include in that package that would make you feel supported that you can get results?"

Question No. 7:

How much would you pay for the package that you just described?

A lot of the time, when you ask people, "How much would you pay to learn about online course creation?" or "How much would you pay to lose your weight?" they give you random prices, like, $10,000, $20,000, $500 or $20, and you can't use them in any way.

However, you can get better responses by asking them about the package first.

Once they describe what they want in a package, then when you ask them how much they would pay, they give you a very accurate price on that. They might say, "If I'm getting eight classes, plus four one-on-ones, plus some templates, plus… plus…, then I am willing to pay $2,000."

Now that's a more realistic answer. It's very important when you are doing this market research you ask Question 6 first about the package and make sure that they give you the answer. Then when you go to Question 7, they can give a price that better matches the package.

Question No. 8:

If I decided to offer this course, would you like to be one of the first students who take this course from me?

Generally, if you hear more than 65% say yes, that means you are on the right path. If you hear between 45% and 65%, you're kind of in a so-so path. If you hear anything less than 45%, you are not on the right path. You have to improve your package, or you have to improve the type of people that you are having conversations with about buying this package.

> **People take courses not because they want to take the course, but because they want to get the results of that course.**

/ヒ—

"Thanks to learning the Ultimate Course Formula approach to planning an online course, I created a course that has so far earned me 48,000 teaching it only three times! I am now applying it to a new course to teach people how to write books. I expect to continue to benefit from the systematic approach I learned from Iman Ag hay. Iman's course is a must if you plan to create online courses."

Pat Iyer
Founder of Report Writing Mastery and
Book Authoring Mastery

CHAPTER 2 (CONTINUED)

Finding People for Your Market Research

Now that you have Iman's 8 Golden Questions, how do we find those eight to 20 people to do the market research with you? We're going to use a couple of very simple social media templates.

- Post them on your Facebook profile

- Post them on your LinkedIn profile

- Go to different Facebook groups and ask the organizer if they are okay with you asking their group members if anyone would be willing to be interviewed.

- Find other leaders who have a following of people in your niche market and see if they are willing to refer some people to you to do this market research.

At the end of an interview, you can ask the person if they know anyone else who is in your niche market (state what it is – like "experts."

You simply need to find eight to 20 people in your target market, and generally, it's not hard to find that many.

If people say to me, "Iman, I can't find eight to 20 people to ask these eight questions," then I say, "Well, you have no business building a course for that market, because if you can't find eight to 20 people who would answer some questions for free, why would you think that they would buy your course from you?" If you can't find eight to 20 people, then you have to question whether or not you should go after that niche market.

Remember, when it comes to the topic and the niche market, each of them should be a maximum of two to three words. In my case, for example, my topic's going to be course creation or online course creation. The niche market is going to be experts.

Also, remember to stick to these templates. Don't change them. Don't add words. Just stick to these questions exactly the way that they are written. They've worked for thousands of my students, and they will work for you.

Template No. 1

Request for people to interview about your topic and your niche.

"Help needed! I'm planning to create an online course about [the topic] (eg.online course creation for experts). I'm looking for 20 people to do a quick 15 to 20 minutes of market research interview on the phone (or on Skype or Zoom). If you are willing to get on the phone with me to do this quick market research, please comment below or PM me. Much appreciated in advance."

That's it. When you post this, people are going to respond. When people respond, you book an appointment with them. The appointment doesn't need to be more than 20 minutes, because those questions should not take more than 20 minutes.

You're going to stick to those questions. You're not going to go into details. You're not going to coach them. You're not going to do any of those things. This is very, very important.

Even if they are making the biggest mistakes of their lives, you are not going to coach them, because the second that you coach them, you are changing the dynamic of that call. These people got on the phone with you to help you with your market research, not to be coached by you. They are going to get the program from you when your course is ready when your package is ready.

After you've had the first post up for a few days, then you can go to the second template.

Template No. 2

"Super excited! I'm planning to create an online course about [the topic] for [niche market]. I'm looking for people who are willing to do a quick 15-minute market research phone call with me. I'm looking for:

People who [have the problem] (e.g., people who are overweight and want to lose weight or people who want to lose 20 pounds in the next 30 days) or...

People who [work with people who have the problem] (e.g., people who help others lose weight).

In either case, end with, "Please comment below or PM me if you know anyone who can potentially help."

With this template, you can first post item 1 above with a specific problem that your target market is facing and the potential result they want to achieve. In the second post, you say the experts who serve the type of people that you want to work with.

For example, I'm doing a course creation course, and another person is teaching experts on how to become a public speaker. Well, most public speakers want to learn how to create online courses.

Let's say in my first message, I post, "I'm looking for experts who want to create an online course," and I get five responses, and nobody else responds, then I can go online again and say, "I'm looking for anybody who is teaching public speaking."

We share the same niche market, but we're not competitors. Those people know many people who probably want to create online courses, so then they can refer those people to me.

Make sure you don't email people the questions in advance. It's very important that you have a conversation with them over the phone. If the person says, "Hey, you know, I'd like to help, but I don't have the time. Can you email me the questions?" Tell them, "No, sorry. This should be a two-way communication because I can ask more questions of you. So, if you can book something, that would be great. If you can't, don't worry about it."

Technically, it's useless if they just fill in the form for you. It's just going to be a waste of your time sending that message. The responses, everything they are going to give you, are going to be wrong. You're not going to get the in-depth answers because there is no interaction

A big part of the market research is that you are building relationships with your potential customers. When they fill out the form, you're not going to build a relationship with them.

That's why it's very important that you get on the phone and talk to them, because a couple of weeks down the road, they're going to be the same people who are going to buy your course from you. Again, it's very important that you do this exactly this way.

Once you find eight to 20 people in your niche market, and you do these eight to 20 market research calls with them, you are going to consolidate all their answers in one file. What does it mean to consolidate the answers? It means that you are going to group all the challenges from all the responders together, all their fears under each other, all their frustrations under each other.

If five people have given you the same challenge, you're going to just write the one sentence, and you're going to add "times five." If you heard the same frustration three times, you're going to put that one down and then write "times three."

This way, you are going to combine the answers, make one file, and you're going to keep that one file as your Client Avatar. That one file is going to give you the language for how you're going to talk to your clients, and how you're going to create a package. That one file will become the foundation of the whole course that you are going to create.

Homework

Start posting these emails online using the templates and share them with your network. Make the appointments and get on the phone, do the eight market research questions with eight to 20 people and then put together your consolidated file.

CHAPTER 3

Module 3-1

Content Structure

So far, you have built your harmonized business model, and you did Iman's 8 Golden Questions. If you've read this far and you're going to study this part without having done the market research, please stop. Go back and make sure that you do the homework before continuing. There is no point in just continuing to read without doing the work.

The work will probably take you three to four hours over the course of a week, so it's not going to take much time, but you have to make sure that you get it done. Otherwise, you won't have the information that you need to be able to do what I'm about to teach you. If you have completed it, let's dive deeper and then see how to put together your content structure.

The purpose of putting together your content structure is always for this one thing – bringing the dream result to your dream clients. Many times, people ask me, "Iman, should we do three-minute videos or five-minute videos or 17-minutes videos or 22-minute videos?" Some people do very short videos around five minutes in length, and some people do longer videos. What's the best model to do?

Honestly, from my point of view, it's not about the length of the video. You can have a three-minute video, you can have a one-minute video, you can do a 17-minute video, or you can have a two-and-a-half-hour video.

Whatever you do, there are going to be some people who are not going to like it. If you do three-minute videos, there are people who will think you're not giving enough information. Some people don't like the one-and-half-hour or two-hour videos because they say, "Well, it's just far too long, and I can't plan for it, I can't do it."

The length of your video is given by the purpose of the content. The purpose of the content is making sure that the students have enough information and enough systems that they can bring the dream result to reality. You want to make sure that your content is digestible. Your content should be long enough that the student can learn from it, but also enable them to get the homework done.

There are many different ways of teaching your content, as well. You can teach it live, or you can record it. If you're teaching your content live, generally you book one-hour sessions, 90-minute, or two-hour sessions to teach your content and do some Q&As. Then you can use the recording of that to give it back to your students.

If you are doing a recorded version of your course, divide the modules into shorter sessions. Although the whole course is going to be the same length, make recorded lessons into shorter portions so if the students want, for example, to study for 20 minutes or 30 minutes, they can grasp that concept, rest, and then come back and continue watching the next video. Just make sure that each module is long enough to give them enough information so that they can take action.

Remember that the most important thing in the whole package you are putting together is making sure the students are getting results by having enough support from you so they can get their work done.

"We always have the best intentions, but things in life come up, and Ultimate Course Formula made it so easy to accomplish. Before UCF, I would stress out about putting together a course, and now I can create one in only a day.

I'm just getting started, and I've already launched over eight courses with five more in the pipeline! The market research was so valuable because I thought I knew my customer well enough to know what they needed.

Now, not only can I attract my ideal client but also repel my less than ideal client simultaneously so that nobody's wasting any time. Having the UCF online community and check-ins was extremely valuable to push me to get things done by providing me with accountability. Iman packages everything with easy-to-follow steps, so I knew exactly what to do and finally understood how to build successful courses! It's always risky when you're taking a new class from somebody, but the amount of value that Iman adds just for the sake of adding value is unbelievable. Iman breaks it down so simply and from a place of integrity, from a place of love, from a place of heart and from a place of giving, and that comes through in everything he teaches. He is out there to help other people and make an impact by inspiring others to go and inspire more people!

If you've been wanting to create a course, and you haven't this course will help you get over some of the limiting beliefs that stand in your way of you actually taking action. Knowing that I can create a course, and Iman's structure on how to put that course out there, super charges my ability to go out and make an impact and for that everyone has the time. If that's your mission, if that's your passion, find a way to make it easy and UCF makes it easy!

If you are on the fence about taking the UCF program and you know that course creation is something that you want to do, just go for it! If creating a course has been a struggle like it was for me, and I needed to find a different way to do it UCF was that different way. It was worth the time; it was worth the investment and it was worth everything because of what I'm now able to do."

Brenda Gardner Jones
Founder at Inspired LIFE Connection

Module 3-2

CHAPTER 3 (CONTINUED)

Online Course Package Options

When it comes to putting together the components of your package and the structure of your content, one of the things you need to understand in the beginning is what are the available options when it comes to your online course creation.

A very common misconception about online courses is that everything related to online courses should be either automated or recorded. To a certain point, there is a truth to that, but that only holds true for courses under $100.

When you are dealing with courses at the qualified or committed level, your package requires you to have a lot more than just content. Then the question is, what are the options and extras that you can include in what type of package?

The first thing you can put in an online course package is recorded videos, recorded audios, PDFs such as blueprints and step-by-step guides, templates, and things like that. A series of recorded pieces of content can be amazing. They give people a lot of information, and that's what we put together as the foundation of any course that we build for interested people.

Anything from free courses to $100 courses can be made up of just this. At this level, no one expects more than just a few pieces of recorded content, such as PDFs and audios.

If you want to take the course to a little bit higher level of value and give your students a bit more support, you can add something called automated emails where you can break up the content. What that means is that you take pieces of the content, put it inside emails, and over time, make those pieces of content available to the students.

For example, let's say you have a weight-loss program and you want to give one exercise a day to your students. You give them one email a day. In that email, they get that exercise of the day.

The next day they get another email. The third day they get another one. You don't want to sit and write one email per day per person in the program; that's ridiculous. There are systems that do that for you automatically.

Often, a question comes up, "Is it good to feed content in pieces to people, or is it better to give access to all the content at once?"

Let's go back to the guideline that the purpose of your course is getting people results. If the best way to get people results is breaking up the content when giving it to your students, then you should break up the content. If the best way to get people results is to give them all the content at once, then give them all the content at the very beginning.

Another way of doing this is that you give all the content to them at once, but you set up Email Automation that reminds them every week or every day, or whatever schedule you are using, to look at a specific piece of the course. That would work as well.

However, even if you add email automation, that still doesn't add much value to your course. It keeps the course at the interested level, and you have more communication with your students, but it doesn't elevate the level of the overall value of the program.

Live Online Instruction

To add value to your course, which instantly takes the course from the interested group to the qualified group, you should include live online classes. For that, we use a tool called Zoom. I highly recommend you become familiar with it, and it's going to be a part of your exercise for this session.

Go to www.successroadacademy.com/zoom to download and install the software. At the time of writing this book, you could use Zoom for free for sessions up to 40 minutes long, which is great. Once you have the software, practice having meetings over Zoom. Try it with different numbers of people if you can, so you get used to doing live classes with different sizes of groups. That will train you to teach your classes live.

To add value to your series of recorded audios and videos, and PDFs, add some live online classes. There are two ways that you can do this:

- Record all your course material and then use Zoom for live online classes that are in a question-and-answer (Q&A) format.

- Have the online videos but then when you go to the weekly classes, you plan those classes over four, six, or eight weeks (whatever works for the amount of material you have) and you teach at the beginning of each of those classes and then do a Q&A in the same class.

In my experience, people love doing it the second way. People like to have a start date and a finish date. They love to show up together in a live class, learn together, and participate in a Q&A.

Then they love to go, do the homework and submit their homework to a Facebook group or other type of group that you have so they can get feedback from you and each other. My students enjoy training the best when it's this way.

This type of package – combining online training, Q&A with recorded materials and group support, can be anywhere from $500 to $2,000. If you're putting together a $97 package, this course design won't work, it's just too much work. However, if you're charging $500 to $2,000, then that package potentially will work very well.

Another option is to teach live online classes via teleseminars. For that, we use a tool called MaestroConference. The reason that you might want to do live online classes via teleseminars is if you are teaching something where the privacy of the students is important. Otherwise, if privacy isn't important in that course, I wouldn't use teleseminars. I would definitely use Zoom over everything else.

Students can also adjust their privacy with Zoom. They can turn off their video feed so people can't see them, and they can make up profile names, so people don't know their real name. So there are lots of privacy features in Zoom as well.

However, let's say you are teaching a course in which you are talking about how to avoid getting hacked. Let's say the students in the course that are showing up live in the classes want to talk about the vulnerabilities in their IT department.

Obviously, they don't want other students to know who they are because the other people on the call will hear about all the vulnerabilities in their system, and that would be a very dangerous thing. The other students could then hack their IT department.

In that case, the privacy of the students becomes extremely important. Using MaestroConference allows people to join the class anonymously. Just their voices can be heard, so it allows them to feel more comfortable discussing their situation.

This can also be important if you're doing something that involves private matters that people might feel uncomfortable sharing. For example, privacy is important if you're teaching a class on relationships for people who have been cheated on, or for people who have cheated on someone. There could be many people who don't feel comfortable being on camera and admitting they cheated on someone. They might want to go through a program dealing with this issue, but they would want to remain anonymous.

The privacy offered using software like MaestroConference makes it easier for people to have conversations than if they were using Zoom.

Added Support for Students

The next piece that you can have as a component of your program is an online support group, and there are two tools that you can use. One of them is Facebook, and the other one is LinkedIn. The one you choose depends on the type of program you have.

If your program is business-to-business, where people who are participating are from corporations, or they're professionals, then using a LinkedIn group may work better. In all other cases, I would suggest using Facebook. You can use Facebook because most people have accounts on Facebook, and they can access and use it easily.

There is also software that exists that allows you to create your own group and training platform. One of those tools is Thinkific, which I'm going to talk about in Step 6.

In addition to online support groups, it can be helpful to have accountability partners. Remember this: courses for interested people provide knowledge, qualified courses provide support, and committed courses provide accountability.

So now, from this point forward, you are moving toward building a committed course. With that, you can give people accountability partners, which means that you will match each student with a support person.

The support person can either be a coach within your program who holds the student accountable, or it can be another student and between the two, they're holding each other accountable.

Generally, if you're looking at providing accountability partners, that starts in courses that are over $2,000, most likely $5,000, $10,000, and above. If you are paying the support person to provide accountability, the course will be higher priced

The next piece you can add for students is one-on-one support. The one-on-one support does not have to be in person; it can still be online. As I mentioned earlier, I'm constantly traveling the world, and sometimes, I do one-on-one support with my one-on-one students.

This way, your program doesn't take away from your location freedom. You can do one-on-ones over the phone, over Skype, over Google Hangout or Zoom.

I use Zoom for pretty much everything in the company, and I use my cellphone as a backup. One of the good things with Zoom is that you can use your phone to call in for access to Zoom. So even if the other person is on Zoom software on their computer, if you don't have a good Internet connection, then you can simply use your phone to call into Zoom and connect that way. You can do one-to- one support once a week, twice a week or every two weeks depending on your package.

Last, but not least, you can include in the packages "done-for-you" (DFY) services. This is only for high-end packages, such as a package of $10,000 or more. You are doing the work for them. You could be building something entirely from scratch. DFY services can be a part of your course or can be the entire package that you offer them.

> *Courses for interested people provide knowledge, qualified courses provide support, and committed courses provide accountability.*

"I have never been involved in training where someone would get me out of the fear and into action mode the way Iman Aghay does it. Honestly! It is like getting right into the crux of the hand through all the obstacles that were there! I am ever so HAPPY, and this method really WORKS!"

Agnieszka Burban

CHAPTER 3 (CONT.)

Iman's Program Success Formula

Besides looking at the components that you can include in your course package, such as recorded videos, PDF's, a Facebook support group, one-on-one support, group support, etc., there is also something called the Program Success Formula.

The Program Success Formula is not something that you sell like features or like the previous components that we talked about.

These components are more intangible but are extremely important. When you put together your package, you want to make sure that these five conditions are met. People need to be able to see or feel that these five things exist in the program before they invest in the program. What are those five things?

A Person to Look Up to

When it comes to your course, it's very important that they can look up to the teacher of their program. On that note, how do you become a person to look up to? There are two ways to do this. The first is for people who have already achieved massive success, and the second is for people who are getting started.

Yes, absolutely, both of these two types of people can become a person to look up to, and you need to know how to become that person.

For the people who have already achieved massive success, to become a person to look up to, it's not about your success story.

It's not about what you are achieving today or how much money you are making today. It's not about what a great life you have either. It is, in fact, it's all about the struggles that you went through that your customers can relate to and the story of how you overcame those struggles to become the person that you are.

When you are living your life, there are so many things that you struggle with, so many challenges, so many fears, so many frustrations that you go through, and there are so many successes that you have. How you choose what challenges, fears, and frustrations to tell in that story, and the dream result that you have to talk about to connect to people and become the person to look up to, is by going back to your market research.

Look at the challenges, fears, and frustrations that your students are dealing with and find a part of your story that relates to those challenges, fears, and frustrations and then looks at the dream result that the students want to achieve and how you are living that dream today.

Remember, the reason that people connect with you is your struggle, not your success.

Some people might think, "Okay, you understand where I am today, and you know how to get to the results I want, so, I can look up to you." That's for instructors who have already achieved results; however, for most of you reading this book right now, you're most likely at the beginning of your journey.

You are at the point where you are saying, "Oh, Iman, but I haven't achieved massive success. I'm not a person whom people will feel inclined to look up to, so how do I become that person?"

As I said, the first way is you achieving massive success for yourself. The second one is becoming a person to look up to because of the results that you have been able to achieve with your clients. That's how most of us start. With the first group of students that we teach, they didn't see any of those results, but they trusted us because we told them right out of the bat that they're the first group of students that we are teaching. That's why we call them the beta group – the test group.

If you go back to what I said in Chapter 1, the first group of people that I taught was a group of eight entrepreneurs, and I taught them marketing. It was the first time I was teaching them marketing, but one of my students went from having 12 people attend his events after 12 years, to being able to do a 540-person event in 45 days.

The result that he got from working with me, that story became the reason that everybody else started looking up to me. They think, "If Iman was able to get this result for this person, then I want to follow Iman. I want to follow what he said." Out of those eight students that I started with, four of them achieved massive success within the eight weeks that I was working with them.

I created that success story of becoming the person to look up to because of the results of my students, not because of the result I achieved. At that time, I had never done a 540-person event. I had never gotten into corporations the way my other students had.

However, I got them the results. In summary, you become a person to look up to either through your own results or through the results that you get for your students.

Now, what do you do if you are starting from scratch? Don't worry about it, because when you're starting from scratch, that's what you tell them. You explain to them, "I'm starting absolutely from scratch. So, the first class that I'm going to teach is my beta group. It's going to be the first group of students, and I'm going to put all my energy, heart, and soul to make sure that you can achieve massive success."

That becomes the exact reason that people want to work with you. That becomes the exact reason that people want to go through your class and get results.

When you are teaching your first class, people don't care about whether you're a person to look up to or not, because what they care about is that you're starting, and they know that they're getting an amazing deal and your dedicated support so they will be able to achieve those results. Can you see that the first time around, you don't need to worry about this at all?

The second time around, because you have gotten amazing results for this beta group, then you can use the success stories from your beta group. That creates a great program for you, and then after teaching it for a couple of years, when you have built a successful life, successful business, or whatever is your dream, then you use your story to inspire people and become a person to look up to because of your success.

A Common Goal to Achieve

One of the greatest things that my students learn from my program is that, with every course that I teach, at the end of every class, I give people specific homework. That homework becomes a specific goal that is common between all my students that all of them want to achieve.

When we are teaching Ultimate Course Formula, in the live format, every week, I teach one step. I have 100 or 200 students going through the program, and then I give them one common goal to achieve. For example, by the end of the week, I want them to complete their market research.

The homework assignment becomes a common goal for everyone to achieve, and that creates a sense of community and a sense of support. Everyone knows that we all are doing it together at the same time, and that fuels their momentum.

When people have momentum in the course they are following; they are far more active in that course compared to everybody else.

A System to Follow

Write this down for yourself somewhere: The biggest challenge your students have is being overwhelmed. Most students who want to achieve certain things can't achieve them because they are overwhelmed with the number of options they have.

They're overwhelmed with the number of distractions they have, so they cannot get results from what they do.

The best thing you can do is create a step-by-step system for the students to do things one step at a time so that they can be less overwhelmed.

Now write this other sentence down for yourself:

Any system is better than no system at all.

What does that mean? That means that, yes, you are beginning your journey and this is the first time, most likely, that you are putting together your system. You haven't used this system before; you haven't tested this system. You just invented the system. You just put it together.

Remember that any system works better than no system at all! So, when you are teaching your students, and you give them a step-by-step system, it will help them get far better results than if they were on their own.

Obviously, you want to create the best system that you possibly can. Based on the market research that you did and doing Iman's 8 Golden Questions, you know the exact challenges, fears, and frustrations they are dealing with. You know exactly what they want to learn and what they want to achieve.

You have the knowledge and power to create this system for your students to get them amazing results. Any system is better than no system at all. When you teach your class for the first time to the test group, you get lots of experience, and based on the results your students are getting, you can improve your package and your system. For example, when I was teaching Ultimate Course Formula three years ago, we never had Iman's Program Success Formula as part of the package. It didn't exist.

Over time, when I started looking at programs that were successful in the market, these five things were common between them, so I added them to my program.

Also, Iman's 8 Golden Questions didn't look like what it looks like today. You improve the system as you teach. My first group of students got amazing results, my second group of students got amazing results, and my current students are getting amazing results compared to not following any system at all.

A Community to Belong to

People need to feel that they are part of a group of community of people who have a shared goal. They want to be with people who care about each other, who support each other, and who exchange ideas so that everyone can achieve the success they want.

Having a Facebook or LinkedIn group makes a big difference in the success of your students. Make sure that if you are creating any course that is higher than the interested group – meaning any qualified course or any committed course, you are building a great community.

For example, in my mastermind, we call it the LEAD family, because it's a family of LEAD members, and as I'm writing this, more than 80 people are in that LEAD family. So, that makes a ton of difference for this group of students When people are going through rough patches in their lives, they come back to their LEAD family, and they can lean on this family. They can get ideas and feedback from them.

Even in the Ultimate Course Formula, we have the community of Ultimate Course Formula students. People in that community support each other, and it provides momentum and motivation that gets amazing results.

A Mindset and Better Environment to Look Forward to

This is probably the biggest shift that many of your clients need to go through. The environment is what causes some of the issues your clients have.

For example, I would say, generally, in most families, where one person is overweight, most likely, there are other people who are overweight. Why?

Because their environment is one of eating unhealthy food or eating too much and, therefore, gaining weight. Your group community should give people a better mindset and a better environment to achieve the results they desire.

When you give people a supportive environment to belong to, when you give people a better mindset to belong to, the ones who want to get results, the ones who care about getting results, will lean on that family. They lean on that community. They recognize that with a better mindset, they will get much better results.

As I said, you're not really selling these five components, but these things should exist in the background of your program.

When you are talking about your program, people can clearly see that you are the person to look up to, everybody is getting a common goal to achieve, there is a system to follow, there is a community to belong to, and, most importantly, there's a mindset and a better environment with people to support them. They can see that when they belong to this community with that mindset and that environment, they can change their lives and their clients' lives by getting better results.

These five components need to be part of the structure of your program to make sure it works really well, and people can get the support and the results from it.

> *The biggest challenge your students*
> *have is being overwhelmed.*

Module 3-4

CHAPTER 3 (CONTINUED)

Naming Your Course

When you're putting together the structure of your content, it's also a good time to start thinking about the name of your program. There are three things you want to consider when it comes to naming your program.

Name your program for credibility

Have a clear name (instead of having an innovative, creative name) Use the three-word naming strategy.

Remember this: You build your credibility with marketing, but you can lose or reinforce your credibility with delivery.

When I say delivery, it means delivering what you promise to people. You can be the best of the best in the market, in doing the certain things that you do best, but as long as you don't market for credibility, you will stay the best-kept secret in your market. When you name for credibility, you are marketing your credibility without using any taglines or having conversations or making any guarantees.

Here's an example. About ten years ago, when I was starting my career, I was an immigrant who could barely speak English, and I was almost 17 days away from becoming homeless. At that time, I started a new group, and I named that group Vancouver Business Network.

Literally, before starting the Vancouver Business Network, I was a new immigrant who could barely speak English, who didn't have any connections or network. After I started the Vancouver Business Network, I became the founder of the Vancouver Business Network, who happened to be an immigrant.

You see how just naming something for credibility gives you massive amounts of credibility instantly, just because you named it correctly? Right now, I have a group called Entrepreneurs International Network.

So, imagine if a person doesn't know me at all, but I'm introduced on stage, and the person that is introducing me says, "Help me welcome the founder of Entrepreneurs International Network, Iman Aghay."

Even if a person in the audience doesn't know me whatsoever, they think, "Wow, he is the founder of Entrepreneurs International Network, so he should be somebody that matters."

Now, when I get on stage, if I present poorly if my content is horrible, then I'm going to lose the credibility. It's not like I can market credibility, and that I'll stay credible for the rest of my life.

To deliver on the things that you've promised, you must deliver on your credibility. If you deliver on your credibility, then you stay credible. That's why we want to use clear names. Clear names build credibility.

When it comes to naming, there are two names that you are dealing with. There is the naming of your company, and there is a naming for your course. Both your course and your company should give you credibility.

For example, the name of my company is Success Road Academy. The reason that we added the word Academy after Success Road is because I wanted to build credibility around my company that we are an actual academy.

We are not just a one-man show, so I didn't want to call it Iman Aghay Coaching. I wanted to give myself credibility, so I built Success Road Academy.

Today, we are living true to that, because Success Road Academy is not just taught by myself; it's an academy of several mentors, coaches, an entire marketing team, a real academy.

That naming is what gives you credibility right away. The name of my course also gives us credibility. For example, Ultimate Course Formula is the ultimate formula for course creation. Again, the name is designed to give us credibility.

There is a technique to creating effective name called the three-word naming strategy. Look at the names Vancouver Business Network, Entrepreneurs International Network, Success Road Academy, and Ultimate Course Formula. All of them are made up of three words.

How do you do that? You have five options when it comes to the naming of anything that you want to do, whether it's your corporation, your company, or your course. These are some of the options that you can use.

Location:

It can be the name of a city, the name of a province, the name of a state, or the name of a country: International, Global, Phoenix, California, or Canada.

Target market:

Moms, entrepreneurs, men, coaches, whatever your target market is. What the course is: It can be a formula, blueprint, a mastermind, a network, a system, etc.

Level of the course:

It can be mastery, 101 or Level 1, beginner's level, advanced, or the ultimate level? What is it?

Topic:

It can be a general topic such as marketing, weight loss, productivity, business, communication, etc. It can also be more specific such as listening, speaking, leading a Zoom call, etc.

Just to clarify one thing, when we talk about the three-word naming strategy, one part of the title might be two words forming one idea — for example, weight loss. Although weight loss is two words, we count it as one word because it is one idea.

A three-word title using the three-word naming strategy could be Ultimate Weight Loss Formula. Ultimate is the level, weight loss is the topic, and "formula" is what the course is.

When you are ready to create your course name, you write your options for each of the five options. Then, start mixing and matching, not worrying about the order. It doesn't need to be target market, then what it is, then level. It can be topic first, then level, then what it is. Or, it can be level, then the topic, then what it is. You can mix and match in any shape or form that you want.

In the end, you want people to be clear about what you are offering so they can tell if it's designed for them.

Let's try some of these words. For example, I'm going to go with the level, and say ultimate, and then go with the topic marketing, and then go with what it is, a formula.

So, Ultimate Marketing Formula. Well, maybe that's one option. I'm going to write it out. Then try Marketing Ultimate Formula. That doesn't work as well.

Now let's try with the target market, then the topic, and what it is. Let's say my target market is entrepreneurs. So I write Entrepreneurs Marketing Blueprint. Hmm, not bad!

Let's try something else, such as Ultimate Entrepreneurs Marketing or Entrepreneurs Ultimate Marketing. Which best expresses the course?

Just write all the options that make sense to you. Then you can choose the one that resonates the most and gives you the most credibility.

Besides the name, we can also have a subtitle. If your name isn't 100% clear, you can also add a subtitle later on, but your subtitle should clarify what the promise of your course is.

For example, the name of my course is Ultimate Course Formula, and the subtitle of my course is How to Create and Sell Your Online Course in 60 Days or Less. That subtitle clarifies the result that is promised.

Module 3-5

CHAPTER 3 (CONTINUED)

Homework

Based on Question 6 that you asked during your market research, it's time to put together the structure of your course.

The people you surveyed told you exactly what package they wanted and the prices that they wanted to pay. Based on that package and the pricing that makes sense, start putting together the features that the course is going to have and the content structure based on what they wanted to learn.

Don't worry about it too much. Don't think, "Oh, what if it's not the best?" because your students are going to give you amazing feedback to improve your course.

The next thing you want to do is choose the name of your course following the three-word strategy we just covered. Then continue doing your market research. If you end up doing 20 interviews, then you can do another 20. Why not?

The more market research you do, the more successful your course is going to be. We want a minimum of eight, but that doesn't mean you can't do 20, 30, 40, or 80. Most likely, after 20 people, you're not going to hear a lot of new things, but because you're getting people to say yes to answering your questions.

At the end of the interview, if they want to know more, and if they may want to buy your course, then you're building a buyers list.

I remember a couple of years ago, I was putting together a course, and I did 125 market research calls. After the 20th one, almost nobody was giving me any new ideas, but at least 125 people wanted to get one of my courses, so I could go back to them, introduce them to the course, and sell the course.

Complete this homework before going to Step 4.

"When I was introduced to Ultimate Course Formula, I had already created a course! However, it was selling the course that I had fallen short on! In my mind, I thought I had to create the sales force myself. As soon as I started Ultimate Course Formula, I resonated with every word that Iman said! He talked about having many experiences that I could look back at my past and go, "Hmm, I have that too. Oh, I have that too. Oh, I have that too." One of the things that he taught us was that we needed to do a market research study. I went, "Hmm, I don't even know what that is. I don't know how to do a market research study." So, I listened, and I learned, and I put together my first market research! Here's the part that was so exciting. As I did my market research, the people I interviewed almost all said they wanted to be part of my beta group! I knew people would've loved the best thing since sliced bread, but I didn't have the sales formula to get that message out to the world!

My long-term goal for this is to create golfers that want to go to the next step in what I'm teaching! My course takes these golfers through a certification program so they can be licensed to teach the system that I've already created. In this manner, I can have many more golf schools with additional Pros teaching for me. I can't begin to thank you enough Iman for Ultimate Course Formula! I have been able to pull this piece of understanding out of the back of my head so that I can put it to work. My program is the Empowered Golfers Formula 90 Day Virtual

Golf School! I am always receiving testimonies about how my program is helping people improve their golf experience! That's a huge present to me. Those kinds of testimonials are the thing that makes you know you're doing the right thing!"

Martha Sue Yeary,
Business is B.I.O.N.I.C. Golf Pro,
Empowered Golfer's Formula

CHAPTER 4

Module 4.1

The Course Guideline

In this chapter, you are going to prepare a course one-pager so you can go out and start offering your course to beta users and start selling your course.

First, let's review a little bit of what we have done so far. In Chapter 1, we created your harmonized business model. That's how you will generate income with your course and how your course is going to work as a part of your marketing strategy.

In Chapter 2, we covered market research with eight to 20 people. Hopefully you have done more than eight people, or even more than 20 people. Now you have built a list of all the people who want to get the course.

In Chapter 3, you put together your course and features.

Now is the time to put everything together in one place, go to the market, and invite people who said yes they are interested in knowing more. You don't know if they're going to buy or not, and that's totally fine, but now is the time to go back to them and invite them to buy the program.

To do that we are going to put together something called the Course Guideline. As part of the Course Guideline, there is a part we call the course one-pager. Just so we're clear, the course one-pager is one part of the Course Guideline. It is the piece that we use for selling the course publicly.

You're going to start the first part of your course one-pager with the name of your program. Write down your program title, and below the program title, you're going to write the subtitle, also known as the hook or the promise of the course. That's what people are going to achieve by the end of this course. For example, Create and Sell Your Online Course In 60 Days or Less.

Sometimes my students will panic about this hook and promise. People ask, "Iman, how can I promise that if they don't do their homework?" Don't panic about this. It's the same, for example, when a car company advertises a car that goes from zero to 60 in five seconds. That doesn't mean that anybody who sits in the car will press their foot hard enough on the pedal to go from zero to 60 in five seconds. If they don't push their car, it's not going to get to 60 in five seconds: it's going to take 20 seconds. It's not that the car can't go, it's that the person isn't using the car to do it.

It's the same thing with your course. In your course, if a person takes the course, studies everything, does the work, and gets the entire benefit of the course, what's the best result they can get? That's the promise of the course.

Now, if a person buys the course and never shows, they're not going to be able to get the promise. It's not your fault; it's that they haven't done the work. So, don't look at the worst clients.

Don't go with a promise for the worst clients because, technically, that's not your fault if they're not doing their work. Go with the promise for the best of the best clients, and that's going to be the promise of the course.

When I say, "Create and Sell Your Online Course in 60 Days or Less", that means:

If a person shows up every week, does their homework, submits their homework, gets the feedback they need to keep moving forward, actively participates in the community, and does everything they are supposed to do, they can use my system to create their online course in 60 days or less.

If they don't show up, if they don't do homework, that's not my fault. I'm not going to go and advertise for the worst client ever.

You've got to market for the best clients, and you've got to encourage them. You've got to give them a system they can use to get the results. Your title will motivate many of your clients because they know that promise is possible since it's in the title.

Self-Qualifying Questions

For the next part of the one-pager, you're going to have three self-qualifying questions. There are a few characteristics for self- qualifying questions. Generally, these questions are the questions that are about the person's feelings – how they feel today or what they want to do. The answers to these questions should be yes, yes, yes. You do not ask a self-qualifying question where the answer would or could be no. The answer should always be yes.

In Ultimate Course Formula, for example, I ask, "Do you want to share your knowledge and expertise on the Internet, change people's lives and build a successful business for yourself?"

First of all, this question is about what they want to do. Second, it's a question to which my potential client is going to answer yes. If they would say no to this, they're not going to be my potential client. Always ask the question in a way that the answer is yes and it's going to be about what they want to do or how they feel.

The second question I ask potential clients is, "Do you want to put together an automated system that brings you actual paying clients on a regular basis?"

Again, the answer to that question is yes. Finally, I ask, "Do you get lost between the tools, technology, and the marketing skills needed to get your online training platform up and running?" That's about how they feel.

How do you come up with these questions? From your market research. Remember in your market research you asked them about their biggest challenges, fears, and frustrations?

Remember that I asked you to write their words exactly the way they said those words? That's why I wanted you to do it because you can now use those words from the market research about how they feel and what they want to do so they know this course is designed for them.

Module 4-2

CHAPTER 4 (CONTINUED)

Your Credibility Builder

The next piece to the course one-pager is a sentence that becomes your credibility builder. A credibility builder is one sentence that clearly tells people why this course is the course they should take. For example, in my case, it says, "Ultimate Course Formula is the world's leading program to show you how to create and build a lucrative business with selling online courses."

Sometimes people say, Iman, wait a second. I'm just starting my course, so what can I say in my credibility builder?

There are two things that I always suggest that my students include in the credibility builder. The first is to have a comprehensive program. People are looking for comprehensive content. People are looking for content that will answer all their challenges about one thing.

For example, I could say, Ultimate Course Formula is one of the world's most comprehensive programs on course creation. Whether you're starting absolutely from scratch, or you've been teaching your course for years, you can make your course comprehensive. That's a really good promise to give.

The second thing you can include is the support you offer students. You can have your course be one of the most supportive courses in the world. Tell prospective students that you will take their hand and help them achieve results, which I highly recommend by the way. Especially if you are teaching your course for the first time as a beta group, you always want to give as much support as you can to your students.

Again, I could say, Ultimate Course Formula is one of the world's most supportive programs in helping students create and launch their online courses within 60 days or less and build a lucrative business around it.

If you have been teaching your material for a while, that can also be included as a credibility builder. You can say your system has been tested with hundreds or thousands of students. As long as the system is the same system, it doesn't matter if you're teaching it online or offline.

Features and Outcomes

After you've created a Credibility Builder for your one-pager, you're going to talk about the features.

These are the features you worked on in Chapter 3. If you haven't done this work, this is going to be very complicated for you to do, so complete it before continuing.

Features can include access to live group coaching calls, online training videos, a support group, whatever you decided to put together as part of your course structure in Chapter 3.

Once you've listed your features, you then want to include your outcomes. What's the outcome of the program? "By the end of this program you will..." and then you tell them about the outcome. It could be, "By the end of the program you will have your membership area fully set up, your first course will be ready to sell, and you'll create your online sales funnel."

One thing to note is that when it comes to the outcome part of the course one-pager, you do not want to use the word "learn" or "discover."

People don't buy your course to learn stuff. If you think about the Ultimate Course Formula, you aren't interested in building online courses. What you want is to get results. In fact, if you could skip reading the book and just have your online course with the snap of a finger, that's most likely what you would do.

Since you can't just snap your finger and have your online course out there, you have to read the book. That means that you don't want to learn how to create an online course; you want to have your online course.

So you're not going to say, "You will learn how to build a membership area" or "You will learn how to put together your first course." Instead, you say, "You will have your membership area set up." "You will have your first course ready." If a student didn't do their work, then that's not your fault. If one of you is reading this book right now and you haven't done the homework of Chapter 2 or 3, that's not my fault.

You market your course for the best student. You don't market your course for people who don't follow the system. You make sure that if they follow the system, they can get results based on your system.

The next thing to put in the one-pager is who this program is for and who this program is not for. How do we define that? Have you ever worked with a student or a client and you wished you hadn't? Have you ever said, "I really don't want to work with this person"? Those are the people who are not right for your program.

For example, for Ultimate Course Formula, people who just want to make money and don't want to give value to people or support people are not the type of students that I want to serve. They are not the type of students that I can help to get any results. For me, this program is for experts who have the knowledge to change people's lives and want to build a successful business for themselves while they're making an impact in the world.

That sentence attracts my best customers to me. That's why we're super excited to work with those students because we know that we can make a huge difference in their lives and I'm excited to go to work every day, see them, hang out with them, and support them to fulfill the promise of this course.

CHAPTER 4 (CONT.)

Setting Up Your Live Course

Now we get to a part that is very important. It is the hidden gem inside this entire Ultimate Course Formula program What I've seen over and over with my students is that they plan to create their online course on their own and they say they want to record their course on a certain date. They get to the date, and they haven't put together their PowerPoint. They're still working on it. Then something gets in the way. They get distracted, and they forget about their course. Two months later, they still don't have their course.

There are lots and lots of fears when it comes to online courses.

- What if the students don't like me?
- What if my content is not good?
- What if my audio is not good?
- What if the technology is not good?
- What if I can't sell my course?

Many fears come up.

There is so much self-sabotage when it comes to course creation. What you want to do is, instead of creating your course as a recorded course, teach your course as a live course. What that means is that you want to sell your course to a few people and give them a specific start date.

For example, you set a very specific start date in three to four weeks. Then you set a time – let's say every Wednesday at 10 a.m. Pacific Time. Select one specific day, one specific time, specify how many sessions/weeks the course will last based on the lessons you created, such as every week for six weeks or eight weeks. Now you have the days and time for teaching your course, and you are ready to sign up students.

However, before you start creating the course, you want to make sure that you're building a course that sells. That's why before you even start working on any content, you go back to the people you interviewed in your market research and show them what you created and say, "This is the course I put together. Would you like to buy it?"

If they say yes, and join the program, then you know that your course can be sold. That's when you are going to start to create the course. Those that say yes are going to be added to a Facebook group or a LinkedIn group and get access to the live classes over Zoom.

If they say no, then you haven't built your irresistible offer yet. So you're not ready to create that course and need to work more on the offer, to make sure the offer is irresistible.

Once you have signed up enough people (even two or three) to be a beta group, you start generating the content. You are going to pre-pare one piece of content per week. If you had one week to prepare one piece of content, could you do it?

Sure, you could do it. If I'm about to teach on Wednesday at 10 PST, I promise you my content will be ready next Wednesday at 10 a.m. PST, because when I have five people waiting for a class, ready to come to the class and learn from me, I will prepare my content.

You prepare one week's content then teach it, and guess what happens? When you teach, the very same students give you feedback. They will tell you what they liked, what they didn't like, and what they found confusing. From their feedback, you can improve the content that you taught for the next time, and you can make your content for the following week much better.

In a way, what I'm telling you is that for you to become an amazing online educator, the best exercise you can do is teach a group of students first.

When you teach the first group of students, you gain a lot of experience. When you get a lot of experience, you make your content better. When you make your content better, you become a better teacher. One thing leads to the other.

That's why we always sell the course to the beta group. Now, sometimes people ask me why someone would buy a course that didn't exist before. I explained this in chapters 1 and 2, but, technically, that's the way that the education industry works. If I have a course that starts in four weeks, and the course helps people achieve results, people who want to take it will take it. They're not going to come to me and say, "Do you have the recording of the course? Can you give me the templates?"

It makes a lot of sense for the first course to not be ready because it hasn't started yet. People understand that. This idea that people wouldn't buy a course because it hasn't been created is just a self-sabotaging idea in your mind that's stopping you from taking action.

There is no truth to that in the market. When people buy an online course in its beta version, they don't care if that course has been previously delivered or not. They know they are the first group of students.

On that note, let's continue to talk about the logistics. You have already set a date, and you're going to set a time. Now how do you choose the price?

How to price your course

When you did the market research in Chapter 2, there were questions 6 and 7 of the market research.

Question 6 was about the package they wanted to buy, and Question 7 was about the price they were willing to pay for that package.

Now that you have put together your package, based on that, go back to that market research and see how much people were willing to pay for a package similar to the package that you put together.

There is a chance that a person has told you, "I'm willing to pay $50", but as you look at that package, it's very different from the package that another person said they're willing to pay $500 for.

In this case, you look at your package. If your package is more similar to the $500 package, then the price is going to be $500.

Is the package more similar to the $2,000 package? Then that's a $2,000 package.

If the value is more similar to the $50 package, then it's a $50 package. That's how you're going to set the price.

To handle any hesitancy a prospective client has, I highly recommend you offer a 30-day money-back guarantee when it comes to online courses. Many people don't take advantage of it, which is great, but if you don't have it, then a high percentage of people won't buy the course.

> *For you to become an amazing online educator, the best exercise you can do is teach a group of students first.*

Module 4-4

CHAPTER 4 (CONTINUED)

Course Content and Steps

U p until now, what we've covered in this chapter can all go into one document. These elements will be put together to create the course one-pager you will use to sell your course.

However, besides these components that you are going to use for selling the course, you are going to have other elements for the course guideline. Those elements are more private. They're for you. You can share them with others if you wish, but you don't have to have them to sell the course.

One of these elements is called program steps. Program steps are like the system, the process that you are using.

For example, in Ultimate Course Formula, we had:

Step 1: Harmonized Business Model

Step 2: Iman's 8 Golden Questions

Step 3: Course Content Structure

Step 4: Create a Course Guideline.

It's a step-by-step system. What are the steps that you are going to follow to get results?

When you are creating your course for the first time, you don't have to have the program steps when you are selling the course. You have to have them when you are teaching it, but for selling, at that point, you don't necessarily need to have them. If you have them, it will help you increase your sales. It will help you explain what the course is going to be about. However, it's not a mandatory piece to have.

Another element is a schedule of class content. When you get to week 1, what parts of the program steps do you want to teach? When you get to week 2, what parts do you want to teach? And so on.

Even if you have this, it doesn't mean it's written in stone. Sometimes, for example, I think I can teach something in 20 minutes, but it goes on for one hour. Sometimes I feel like something needs 90 minutes to explain, and it takes only five minutes. Before you teach the material, you won't know.

The final element is any extra online training that needs to be recorded. If you want to record a lot of online videos and other material to complement your online course, you need to have a list of things that you want to record.

As with the other elements, it can be part of the course guideline, and it helps you have a better idea about the program, but you don't need to have them to be able to sell the course.

Module 4-5

CHAPTER 4 (CONTINUED)

Homework

Your homework for this chapter is to prepare your course one-pager. If you've done your homework to this point, you should have everything you need.

Contact the people with whom you did your market research and who said they would like to know more about your course.

Book an appointment with them. Try to do that appointment with over Zoom. It gives you experience using it, and it gives them experience if they are not familiar with it. You can also see their response to what you present to provide additional feedback besides their verbal response.

On Zoom, you can share your screen with them, and you can show them exactly what the course is going to look like using your course one-pager. Or, if you can't do it on Zoom, you can email them the course details shortly before the call. Then, when you get on the phone, you make sure you walk them through the course details.

When you get on the Zoom call, you say, "Thank you very much for doing the market research with me a few weeks ago. I really appreciate it. I did the research with 20 other people. Based on the feedback that I got from everyone, I put together a course that I think will address all the key concerns people identified. I want to share the course with you, get your feedback, and see if you're interested in taking it with me. I'm going to go through every piece with you one step at a time, and I want to get your feedback about each piece.

First, I'm planning on naming the course Ultimate Course Formula. What do you think about the name? Do you think it's clear? Do you think it's a good name? Do you have any feedback? Is there anything I can change about it?"

As they give you some feedback about it, write it down, because that's the best feedback anybody can give you. Why? Because these are your actual customers.

Now, you're not going to take action on every single person's feedback. If you talk to five people and four of them are giving you the same feedback, then you should listen to them.

You have to write down their feedback to learn from them. After you tell them your title and get feedback, you tell them your hook, subtitle, or promise, ask them what they think. Write down their feedback.

Then, you get to the qualifying questions. You say, "So the answer to this question should be yes for you, and I want to make sure that it really speaks to you, and it is addressing the challenges, fears, or frustrations that you gave or it's addressing the things that you want to do. Are there some more important things that I could ask you that you could say yes, this is a good course for me?"

Then, you show them the credibility builder and get their feedback on that. Then, when you show them the features, you ask them, "Okay, what do you think about these features? Are these enough? Do you feel that if you go through the course, you will be supported enough that you can get results?"

Then you go to the outcome – who the program is for and who is it not for? Get their feedback on logistics and prices. You get feedback on all those pieces.

Now that you've gotten your feedback, then you move to the next part of this call. This is a very important sentence. You say, "I truly appreciate that you gave me feedback on the course. Based on your feedback, I think this is going to be a really good course. As you see in the logistics, I'm planning to launch the first group on this specific date, and for the first group of students who are going to take the course, I'm offering a 50% discount. Would you like to be one of the first students at a 50% discount?"

If it's $1,997, "Would you like to be one of the first students at $997?" or "If the price is $997, would you like to be one of the first students at $497?"

Do you have to give them a 50% discount? No, you can give them a 90% discount, or you can give them no discount at all. However, based on my experience, a 50% discount is the right thing. You never want to give them the course for free.

Well, that's not true. You don't want to go and give your course away for free to everyone.

You may hand select a couple of people who are strategic partners and say this person has a big mailing list in my niche market so if I teach the course for free to this person, then I'm going to receive a good testimonial and potentially many referral clients. Strategically, it's a good decision to have that person in the program for free.

Generally, you don't want all your beta group users to end up being free users because you want to make sure that people buy your course. That's very important. You want to keep selling the course at a 50% discount. Based on my experience, do I think that people will buy your course? Absolutely. We have had amazing results for our students who sold the course.

We have students who sold $27,000 worth of yoga classes in eight weeks by using this very same method. We had a person who sold $32,000 worth of real estate investment classes in eight weeks.

Hundreds of my students have proven that this model works and we can get results. If you have this fear in your mind coming up and saying, "Oh no, this can't be done, there's just too much, why would people want to buy?" Trust me and trust the process.

Go ahead and start booking your appointments, get on the calls, and if people are not buying the course, learn from their feedback, improve your course one-pager, and go to the next person and improve your course one-pager and then get more feedback. Then go to the next one and the next one.

As I said, one time, I did 125 market research interviews. I showed my course one-pagers to more than 125 people until I got the course right, but then I sold 22 packages at $2,500. At first, none of them bought the course, but I kept going, kept going, kept doing market research, and as a result of that I was able to create a $2,500 package that 22 people bought with this same strategy and tactic I am teaching you here.

That's your homework. You're going to go out there, set a start date, and start selling your course. I would suggest to set the start date for anywhere between three and five weeks from today and then start getting on the phone and selling your course. You want to give people enough time to clear their schedule so they can be in the program.

"What a blessing it has been to take Ultimate Course Formula. I am reaching hundreds of people now that I would not have reached before if I had not taken the course. I am beyond grateful. Thank you for your confidence in me and your support!"

Marilyn Sutherland
Free to Create

CHAPTER 5

Module 5-1

Setups for Recording Your Course

So far in the program, you've put together your Harmonized Business Model and you've done Iman's 8 Golden Questions, you've put together your content structure, you've put together your course one-pager, and, hopefully, you've sold your course.

If you haven't done any of that work, or even parts of that work, please go back and catch up. It's going to take you so long to build your course if you haven't sold it and if you don't have students in the program.

There is a chance that you will create your whole course and nobody will buy it from you. Remember that you are not supposed to skip any steps. You have to make sure that you sell your course first before you start creating your course.

If you have done the work, then you're probably excited because you know that you have students signing up and people are giving you feedback. Now is the time to start recording your content.

Let's talk about how to record the content and what technology to use, the different setups you can have, and the features and benefits of each of the technology options.

There are three main ways to create a course. The first is to record your live group classes, the second is studio recordings, and the third is a combination.

For all three, you will need to prepare guidelines, handouts, documents, and other support material. It doesn't matter if you are doing a recording of live group classes you are teaching via Zoom, or if you are doing studio recordings. Either way, you will need to have the documents and handouts and prepare any guidelines before getting into the class.

The difference is that when you're doing the recording of live classes and you are teaching one class every week, you only need to prepare the content for that week, not all the content at once, which is why I like teaching that way. It gives me one whole week to prepare my content.

If you are doing a studio recording and you want to do it all in one go, you need all the content in advance, so it will take you much longer. That's why I always suggest the first time you teach your course do a beta group and teach your classes live on Zoom, which allows you to record everything.

Then, after the live course is finished, you can do a studio recording because, at that point, you have your entire content written. You can also have a combination of both with some parts of your content already recorded from your live class and some parts that you will record afterward.

Recording Live Classes

Let's talk about recording live group classes. There are different ways you can record these. I've talked about doing the classes through Zoom and recording the content using the Zoom software, but there are other ways to get a live class recording.

One of the best ways is to do a live event in person, hire a videographer, and record what you teach. You record the whole day, and that's your course. Then you get the full videos chopped into smaller sections, based on different modules or based on the sections between breaks. You can do a one-camera shoot, or you can do a multi-camera shoot. If you do a one-camera shoot, and each lesson is recorded separately, at the end of the day you have all your course videos.

Many years ago, I was running a search engine optimization (SEO) and web design company. When I decided to stop doing SEO, one of my students in my mentorship programs said, "Why don't you teach people how you do SEO?"

Because I was good at SEO, I put together an event where I said, "I'm going to share all the information that I have on how to build a successful search-engine-optimization company."

Within 14 days, 22 people bought $500 tickets to come to that training. Immediately, I made $11,000 in 14 days by offering to teach people how I do what I do. I hired a videographer, and I put the videographer in the back of the room with just one camera.

I said, "In every module that I teach, you just record that module and then separate the module by stopping the video and then starting the video," so that way I avoided the need for any editing. I prepared a PowerPoint, all the content, and everything. Then he sat in the back of the room, and he recorded the entire content.

As a result of that, we created 22 modules. I paid the videographer $300. It cost me about $200 for the room rental, and I made $11,000 just from selling the course live. So, I had made already $10,500 profit on this. That was only the beginning. Then I put the course online.

Every week we were selling between one and three packages at $300. Every week, I was making anywhere between $300 and $1,000, some weeks more, from selling this online course for years.

Can you see how anyone can easily create an online course by simply teaching a one-day live event and dividing that live event into smaller sections? That's why I say many times people make the creation of their online course far more complicated than it should be. It really shouldn't be that complicated.

The second way to record your course in person is by working with a smaller group of, say, eight or 10 people in a smaller room.

With a smaller group, you don't even need to hire a videographer, use a camera like the Logitech C920. Run the webcam directly to your computer. Then use a microphone that records high-quality audio, such as a Yeti Blue. Then, you just run the class, and press start and stop to record each lesson separately. You record the whole class. That's all you technically need for recording small group classes.

Often, for my mastermind groups, I create small events. I just set up my Logitech C920 and my microphone. That saves a lot of time and energy. That's another very, very simple way of recording content.

My mastermind students care more about the content than the style or quality of the recording, so the recording is more informal.

The final way to record live presentations is to do webinars and teleconferences and record those classes online.

Often, when we say "live," people think that means in person. Live doesn't mean in person. Live can be online or in person. I have a course that runs for a few weeks. Every week we simply go online, I teach the class, and I record the class live online.

These recordings create an archive of classes, and we sell that archive of classes as one of the packages at Success Road Academy.

Studio Recordings

Another way of recording the classes is a "studio" recording. Although you're not necessarily in a studio, it's called a studio recording because you're sitting in front of the camera and you're teaching.

With a studio recording, you don't have other participants. It's just you or maybe you and another content provider, but you're not going to run the studio recording as though you have other people attending the class or as though you are attending a live event.

This studio recording can have different setups and different formats. One of the formats is called the live-person format.

The live-person format can itself have different setups. One of them is the whiteboard recording. With a whiteboard recording, technically you have a whiteboard, you put your camera right in front of it, and you teach on the whiteboard, and you're just recording yourself by the whiteboard. If you are going to do whiteboard recording, I highly recommend you get a very thick marker so people can see what you're writing.

Something else that you may want to consider, instead of using a whiteboard, is using a flip chart. The reason for a flip chart is because whiteboard reflects the light back. So, if you put your lighting in front of the whiteboard, it reflects the light back on the camera, so that people can see the lights. It will be harder to read. However, if you use paper, like flip chart paper, the light won't be reflected back, so it will be much easier to read.

The other way that you can do a studio recording is by doing a sofa or bookshelf recording. This is when you are sitting on the sofa or in an armchair, and you have something like a bookshelf or other object in the background. Those are the types of recordings that you do in a place that feels homier, more comfortable.

Similar to the "sofa" recording, there's a fireplace setup, where you have a fireplace beside you. It creates a more intimate feel and a much more heartfelt connection.

The next recording to consider is sitting at an office desk or using green, blue, or white screens. You can set this up in your home, and you build a proper studio. You may have seen some of my videos when I'm in my home studio. I have a standing desk that goes up and down, so I can stand up, or I can sit down and record my content.

I have a very bright lighting setup in my studio as well. When I built my studio about four years ago, I was mainly home. Now, I'm constantly traveling the world, so most of the time I'm not even home. I've recorded my content anywhere I can, and I've never had anybody complain.

Regardless, having a studio is nice because you get a good background. I suggest if you want to do studio recordings, get a white screen instead of getting a blue or green screen because if you are using a blue screen or green screen, then you will need to edit them out and it will take more time.

The moment that you have to use the editing software, doing recordings gets way more complicated. It takes so much time to edit content. I'd much rather re-record a 30-minute video than editing a 30-minute video to cut two minutes out of it. I'd much rather do the whole thing from scratch than edit the whole thing.

Sometimes I use a professional videographer, and even for those times, I would much rather redo it than have the videographer edit everything and send it back to me because I know it's going to take much longer than if I just take the 30 minutes and re-record it.

Finally, you can also try an outdoor recording. You'll have more challenges to deal with when you're outside. You might have to deal with wind, dogs barking, people in the background, etc.; however, outdoor recordings are always a lot of fun.

I hope this discussion on doing recordings shows you how easily you can create content, any place. That's how you can record live classes. You can do pretty much any setup, as long as you have the right tools.

Screencasts

The next type of recording is a screencast. A screencast is a video recording of the screen while you are live, which is what I do when I teach online. If I'm traveling and staying at a hotel, for example, I'm doing two types of recording at the same time.

On camera, I'm sitting in front of the pool in a good-looking place, but then I'm also doing the screencast. One of the easiest ways to do this if you have Internet access is by using Zoom. I can be in the middle of Central America, for example, as long as there is a good Internet connection, I can go on Zoom and record on Zoom.

Now, the challenge with this method is that if my video is big, then it wouldn't be super high quality because the quality of the video decreases if the Internet connection isn't very fast. Also, the audio may end up being a little bit choppy, as well.

If you are in your home studio, and you have a good Internet connection, then you want to do a screencast. When you record a screencast while using Zoom, you will get both video and audio files at the same time, which is a really good thing. The video of it can be used for your online course.

You can offer the audio file for students who missed the class or want to listen when they don't have access to audio, like when they are driving or working out. The audio files can also be turned into your podcast or, into an audio training. The video plus audio option is another reason why you need to use Zoom.

The next part we need to look at is creating presentations on PowerPoint. The way this works is with a software called Thinkific. You cannot do this with everything. Normally, I'm sharing a PowerPoint with my class, and PowerPoint works with any software. I'm usually using Zoom.

On Thinkific, there is a feature where you can create a PowerPoint with fewer than 20 slides. That's very important. It must be fewer than 20 slides. Save that PowerPoint as a PDF, and then you upload the PDF to Thinkific.

Then on Thinkific, you can go and add audio to every slide. It's one of the greatest ways of creating online courses, especially for people who don't like the type of setup that I have. They may want it to be very professional looking and have everything planned down to the detail. They tend to be strict in the way the content looks. For those people, using PowerPoint and turning them into PDFs, it works very well.

You can also make your PowerPoint slides into a downloadable PDF that people can use while watching the video or listening to the audio. It supports people who are visual learners.

The Combination Production

A combination production is when you use one larger piece of content, then turn that piece of content into many other pieces of content.

Generally, with a combination production, you want to start from the source of the content, and the best source of content is live training – either a live in-person training or a webinar.

Let's say, for example, I want to do a webinar. That webinar can be recorded, which turns it into a video. That video can be uploaded to YouTube or Facebook, or it can become part of my course.

As a webinar, I can separate the audio from the video. So now, on the audio side, I can get that recording, let's say it's an MP3, and make it a podcast. That audio file can then get transcribed. Now I have the transcription of it, which is in text format. That text can turn into several blog posts.

Those blog posts can be added together to become a book. People can read those books, plus they can be divided into smaller sections, and go to digital magazines or Kindle books. Not only can people read the content, but I can turn the book into an audiobook.

Now you see how by creating just one piece of content on a webinar, I can have video, audio, a written transcript, blog posts, books, digital magazines or eBooks, and audiobooks. That's why we call it a combination production.

"I was at a point in my career where I was thinking about giving up on this industry and doing something completely different. I worked behind the scenes both paid and as a volunteer, for many of the bigger people in the industry, and I felt that some of them don't have much integrity. They just want your money. They stand up on stage, they preach their offers, but at the end of the day, many of them don't care about their students. I've had a Facebook Ads agency for a long time. We do funnels, copywriting, and ads.

My next step was going to be on stage as well as speaking and creating courses. I didn't have a mentor to look up to or a method to get the things done that I wanted to do in my business. I started Ultimate

Course Formula. Having already helped create and launch courses for others, I was already familiar with many of the concepts, but I had never heard them so simplified. I chose to take the step forward and implement the formula into my business! I'm location independent now!

I don't live anywhere, I've traveled around the world, for the past two years, working digitally from wherever I am. As long as I've got my laptop and WiFi, I'm good to go! Before Ultimate Course Formula, I felt like my business was a chore. Now I am excited to help people live the freedom lifestyle they want to live through my group, "Freedom Navigators," and my course, "Passport to freedom!" I'm so extremely grateful I took a chance on Iman and Ultimate Course Formula!"

Debbie Peck
Freedom Navigators

Module 5-2

CHAPTER 5 (CONT.)

Recommended Tools

One of the most important things that will make your life ten times easier when it comes to your course creation is using proper tools.

Early in my business and even now, I wasted so much money on buying the wrong tools and investing in the wrong systems, until I figured out the best tools to use. Here is a quick rundown on some of the best tools for your course creation. You can get a lot of this equipment on Amazon.

A Proper Camera

The most important thing you will need in your business is a good camera, but you don't have to spend $2,000 or even $500 on a camera because most of the pieces of your course are going to be delivered online. So as long as the camera records 1080 HD, you should be good to go.

In this case, I suggest that you use a camera webcam called Logitech C920 or C930. C930 is a newer version of C920, but I prefer C920 because C930 records higher quality than 1080 HD, and technically the files are going to be too large. It's going to be hard to transfer them to different places, and at the end of the day you're going to transfer everything at 1080 HD anyhow, so there's no point in getting the C930.

You can probably get the Logitech C920 for under $100, and it directly connects to your computer. Everything you record is going to go directly to your computer without the need for a file transfer and, without the need for heavy editing.

The camera that I'm using most often is the Logitech C920; however, when I'm using Zoom for recording, it decreases a little of the quality when my picture is full screen. It's not because of the camera. It's because of Zoom.

A Proper Microphone

The second thing you want to get is a good microphone, and there are two good microphones that you can get. The Yeti Blue is a really good microphone, especially if you want to record your events. If you have a small group event, you can put the microphone in the middle of the room, and it picks up everybody's voice.

Yeti Blue does an amazing job. When I'm back home, and I'm recording in the studio, I always use the Yeti Blu. I mount my Yeti Blue standing on a hydraulic arm, so it decreases noise from movement on my desk.

You can usually find a Yeti Blue for about $150. Yeti Blue has two versions. There's a professional version and a non-professional version. For most course creators a non-professional version is all you will need.

The other microphone that I like is PowerDeWise. A PowerDeWise is a lapel microphone. Lapel microphones have a holder that you attach to the collar of your shirt or lapel of a jacket, and they record really good quality audio. If I am outdoors and using a Yeti Blue, you would hear a lot of wind noise and maybe other sounds, but when I use a lapel microphone, it's canceling all the background noise, or maybe 99% of those sounds.

That's why I like the PowerDeWise microphone. The other thing about PowerDeWise is that it comes with a very long cable, which allows you to stand away from your laptop and gives you a lot of flexibility to move around.

The PowerDeWise also has a good connection to the computer, but you can also use it with your cell phone. It's a good thing to be able to have a microphone that works with your cell phone and also works with your computer.

Yeti Blue works with your computer, but it doesn't work with your cell phone, because Yeti Blue is a USB microphone. The PowerDeWise works perfectly with your computer and cell phone, and it's only $20.

One thing to know, though, about PowerDeWise is that when you connect it to the sound system of your cell phone or your computer because it goes into the headset jack of your computer, you won't to be able to hear if you want to use the computer speaker.

You would have to remove the device to be able to use the speakers. What you can do is buy a converter that gives you an option to use a headset. And, then one part of it connects to your headset, and the other one goes to your lapel microphone.

The next helpful tool is a cell phone holder that clips onto your desk and has a long, flexible neck. It's very easy to manipulate and put in the place you want to direct your cell phone, so it makes it easy to record on your phone. At the time of writing, Breett sold one on Amazon for about $20.

Proper Lighting

When it comes to lighting, there are two types of lighting that you can get. The first is a ring light. Ring lights come in different sizes, and I would suggest a Neewer brand 18-inch, 55-watt, 5,500K dimmable LED. Again, you can get that on Amazon. If you just want to buy one piece of lighting, that's a great piece to have.

Another type of lighting that you can use for a studio is a dimmable bi-color LED with a U-Bracket. You would usually use that for lighting up your background, and you can use it to light yourself as well, but that's taking it to the next level.

Generally, what you want to do with your lighting is have one light in front of your face, above, one light to the right that lights up the right side of your face as well as your background so it kills the shadows, and one light to the left that lights the left side of your face and your background.

Now, as you know, I always talk about how to have a setup that can make your life ten times easier and one of the devices I bought that has made a huge difference is a cell phone case called the LuMee.

It comes with its own selfie lighting. When you click on one button, the front face of the case starts lighting up, so it gives you really good lighting for your face, and then when you press it again, it gives you great lighting in the background.

This is good to have when you need portable lighting, and it's at night, and you're just in the middle of nowhere. You want to record your content right away. You don't have access to a studio or anything like that. Having a cell phone case that is always with you and allows you to record your content even in the darkest places possible is helpful.

LuMee also has another external light which acts as an external battery as well. I like that device. It takes a little longer to charge, but it's worth it, and I carry one with me anywhere that I go.

It acts as a power bank, and it also acts as a light, so the combination of the LuMee case with that external lighting and the battery charger is just an amazing set of features to have.

Editing Tools

When it comes to video editing, as I said before in the previous chapters, I don't like the videos to be edited. The reason for that is because as soon as you edit the videos, it's going to take so much longer to create your course, and you want to create your course as fast as possible. If you really want to edit your videos, there is a synchronous software called Camtasia for PCs. If you're using Mac, you can use Final Cut Pro, or you can use iMovie, which comes with your Mac.

If you want to do audio editing, there's a software called Audacity. That software is free but try to download it from a reliable source.

Again, I don't recommend editing audio when you can simply use Zoom to record your videos, and it automatically gives you an audio file.

Audio editing software is for people who want to create audio books or an audio course, and you don't want to use Zoom for whatever reason. Then that's the day you would go to Audacity. However, I would still stick to Zoom and get the audio file from Zoom.

The next thing to look at is a webinar tool for selling. I would suggest you use Webinar Jam. It's a super tool for one-way webinar communication when you want to present your content and close the sale without people interrupting you during the presentation. If you want to have two-way communication for educational purposes, then you want to use Zoom.

In summary, I think the best tools that you need to create and sell your online courses and record your material are Zoom to run the course and record the audio and video, a PowerDeWise microphone to record the audio, the Yeti Blue for live course studio recordings, and the Logitech C920 to record the video.

Last but not least, you may want to outsource any graphic design, video/audio transcriptions, or other technical work. For that, you can go to fiverr.com. Search for graphic design, logo design, whatever it is you need, find a person, and they will get the work done pretty quickly.

Make sure that you read the reviews and make sure that you clearly define the description of the work that you are ordering, but it's pretty straightforward using Fiverr.

"Ultimate Course Formula has been a great experience! Since starting Ultimate Course Formula, I have successfully launched three courses: "Ultimate Horse Training Formula," "Ultimate Goal Setting Formula for Equestrians," and "Clicker Training Mastery."

Now, I also do my courses on Zoom where we can interact face to face, and I use FaceTime. That changed everything for my business. I know how to share screens and have wonderful visuals! I was missing the funnel piece in my business.

Through Ultimate Course Formula I was able to complete that final piece of my business to make it more successful! My business, Hippologic, has been helping many equestrians make horse training easier through my online courses, and I am extremely grateful for Ultimate Course Formula!

Sandra Poppema
Hippologic

Module 5-3

CHAPTER 5 (CONTINUED)

Homework

The homework for this week is, first, to continue selling your course and doing more market research if you need to. That market research, as you know, is not just market research, it's part of the sales process.

The second part is to put together some content for a smaller course. Now, technically, what I want you to do is to get comfortable with recording your content. I've given you this homework before.

I'm going to remind you again, that if you haven't put together a small meeting on Zoom, I highly recommend you put together an event with a few people coming together on a Zoom call. Confirm them, give them the Zoom link, and then have a meeting with them. Record that conversation so you can see how Zoom works, and that will help you a lot with putting together your content.

Third, I want you to go to your PowerPoint program, create a short presentation, fewer than 20 slides, and save that PowerPoint as a PDF. The way that you do that is to click on "Save As" and select "Save as PDF" from the drop-down menu. Once you have a PDF, you can use it to practice uploading it to a membership site like Thinkific, which I will talk about in the next chapter.

When you're certain about the name of your course, get your logo done. You can go to Fiverr or go to any graphic designer. The logo should be in transparent PNG format. That will help you a lot if you have those files ready when you come to the event with us to build your sales funnel, your membership platform, and your membership training center.

CHAPTER 6

Membership Platforms

The sixth step in creating and selling your online courses is to build your membership platform. Your membership platform is the online website where you upload and secure your content. It's the place where you can manage your students, see who has purchased your courses, how many timese each student has logged in, and how they have progressed in the course. You can also use some membership platforms to sell your courses, build your sales page, and even create affiliate links or promotional codes to track your affiliates.

When it comes to membership platforms, the technology has improved so much over the past few years that almost anyone with basic computer knowledge can build their membership platform.

The key is to choose the right platform. The membership platform that I recommend is Thinkific. The good thing about Thinkific is that it allows you to have all the following functionalities in one tool:

- Video hosting
- Document hosting
- Multimedia hosting
- Payment processing integration

- Upfront payment, payment plans, and subscription type user management.
- Affiliate tracking
- Landing page builder
- Sales page builder
- Integration to other platforms directly or through Zapier

Zapier allows you to use one tool to completely build your entire membership platform, and even sales funnel. However, I also believe that to get the best result; you need to use every tool for its intended use.

Although you can use Thinkific for building your entire sales process in addition to your membership platform, I suggest you use Thinkific mainly for building your course area and using ClickFunnels for building your sales funnel. Although using the two tools increases your monthly costs, it gives you a lot more capability than you would get with either one alone.

Since I refer many clients to Thinkific, my students and the readers of this book can get an amazing deal by following my affiliate link: http://SuccessRoadAcademy.com/thinkific

The pro version of Thinkific is $97/month, but by following the link, you can get three months of Thinkific for free.

Since Thinkific is an ever-changing and ever-improving tool, I won't be able to write a guideline for it inside the book. However, when you sign up for Thinkific through my link, you'll get specific step-by- step instructions on how to use it and get the most out of the program.

CHAPTER 7

Module 7-1

The Webinar Funnel

This chapter is all about creating your funnel, but let's review quickly about what we've done so far.

In Step 1, we built a Harmonized Business Model.

In Step 2, we started doing market research and Iman's 8 Golden Questions. You talked to many people to understand what people want to buy.

In Step 3, we put together the content structure looking at the pieces we want to offer. What are the components? What are the features of those pieces?

Then in Step 4, you put together your course one-pager, started going back to your beta group, and started selling the course. By now, you should have a few clients. You are starting to build your course. You know exactly how to build a course, based on, Step 5, using Zoom and based on the tools that I introduced to you. In Chapter 6, we talked about how to secure your content on Thinkific.

By this point, you should have been able to launch your beta group, you have students who are going through the course, or your beta program is about to start in the next few weeks.

From this point on, we will focus on building your sales funnel. As I mentioned before, building the sales funnel has a lot of technical parts to it.

Components of a Webinar Funnel

To build your webinar funnel, you need to understand the pieces that make up the funnel. You start with a free webinar, which you invite people to attend. The webinar is anywhere from 45 to 90 minutes, and at the end of the webinar, you invite people to buy your full course.

That's the way that you use a funnel to sell your courses to many people. You can run Facebook Ads, get affiliate partners, and do many things to market yourself. However, for all those, you need to have a system. People will say, "Iman, I built a course, and I want to do Facebook Ads." I always ask, "So what's your funnel?"

Because if you're going to do Facebook Ads, your ads should lead people to a funnel. If you don't have a funnel, all that marketing will be wasted. The funnel you will create is the webinar funnel that we're building for you at the live event.

What are the pieces that make up a webinar funnel? The first component is made up of several webinar invitation emails. They are also referred to as a swipe copy or swipe files for JVs (joint venture partners). You need to write two to three invitation emails for JVs to promote your webinar. I'm going to give you examples of those.

When your JVs who are promoting you sending an email to people on their mailing lists, the recipients click on the link that's inside the email, and they go to your webinar landing page. That's the place people sign up to your webinar.

They go to your webinar landing page, they look at the webinar, and they say, "Yes, I'd like to join the free training." They enter their name and email, and they are put on your mailing list. Once they sign up, they become part of your interested group, so that builds your mailing list.

If they register a couple of days before the webinar, they will get reminder emails leading up to the presentation. Then on the day of the webinar – let's say the webinar happens on Wednesday, 10 – they'll receive an attendance email in the morning that says, "Hey, we have the webinar later today, don't forget to attend." Then an hour before the webinar starts, they get another email that says, "The webinar is today in one hour, so make sure you don't miss it." That's how you get webinar attendance.

Depending on how you set up your system, you will either do live webinars with Webinar Jam or Zoom, or you can do automated webinars with Everwebinar.

In the webinar, people are given a link to click on if they are interested in purchasing your product. That link takes them to the offer wrap-up page, where they purchase your services, your programs, and your product. It's also called your sales page. For people who buy the course, you will have a funnel for delivery of the service, program, or product that will follow.

For people who didn't buy the course after the webinar, they're going to receive something called the post-webinar follow up series of emails that essentially says, "Hey, you attended the webinar, but you haven't purchased the course, and the deadline for the exclusive offer is coming... Buy it now before it expires!"

Last but not least, for everyone who attended the webinar or missed the webinar, they also receive a link to the webinar replay page.

"I was a hot mess. I had a business, and I had mentors to help me with my business. I had been working in and on my business for over 30 years, and I was getting by. I noticed that people younger than new, people newer in business were apparently crushing it, standing on their own stages and doing amazing things in the world, and I was still struggling. This was not pretty.

Being older, more experienced, and less successful led to stress, and my background is as a stress management consultant, so I felt like there must be something wrong with me and I just wanted to hide. It's hard to be successful when you're hiding. Tech scared me. The internet was not something that I was comfortable using to grow my business. I heard Iman Aghay speak at an event about his Ultimate Course Formula. I was like, "Yeah, right. It's not that easy to do an online course and to sell it - in eight weeks."

Iman offered a truly compelling guarantee, and I decided to try it. At this point, I felt like I had nothing to lose because I was investing five figures a year, sometimes multiple five figures a year, in coaches and consultants and tech and trying to get somewhere and feeling like I wasn't getting anywhere.

Fast forward, four weeks into Ultimate Course Formula, I had the structure done. I had my target market. I had my language. Five weeks in, I had my first sale. Six weeks in I had my second sale. Before the 8-weeks was completed, I had revenue more consistently with my online course than I had with my in-person sales.

Now my business is simple, easy to understand, and more profitable than ever. You'll find me simply inviting people to my online course. In my online course, they get what they need, and I know where it's going to lead. Because of that one course, my business has grown, developed, and evolved, right along with my clients. Every client still starts with that one online course that I developed during the Ultimate Course Formula! Thank you, Iman."

Jackie Simmons
Success Journey Academy

Module 7-2

CHAPTER 7 (CONTINUED)

Pre-Webinar Invitation Emails

The first step of the webinar funnel that kicks off the process is made up of the webinar invitation emails. These are the emails that your joint venture partners send out to their mailing lists to promote your webinar.

As I previously mentioned, JVs are people who have a mailing list in your niche market and would like to promote you to be able to sell your course and then get a percentage of what you make from the people on their mailing list.

We're going to talk about how to get JV partners in Chapter 8, so don't start worrying about how you can find joint venture partners. You are not there yet. You will have to create your funnel first before being able to go and get joint ventures.

The first email gets sent out three to five days before the webinar. The subject for the email is usually the webinar title.

My suggestion for your webinar title is to use or the subtitle that you created for your course one-pager in Chapter 4 or your promise or the hook if it's slightly different.

Also, remember that you put together three self-qualifying questions for your course one-pager. Those three self-qualifying questions will be used in the email. ("Do you want to share your knowledge...", "Do you want to have better relationships...")

Then you put, "Register for this free live webinar here." You then include the webinar link.

Then you say, "Join us on this upcoming webinar, and learn how you can...," and then give them the promise. You'll talk about the three things they're going to learn in the webinar, and give them, again, the webinar link.

After that, include your bio and why people should attend the webinar. You'll sign it "Best" with the name of the joint venture.

As you will see, these emails are pretty straightforward. These are the templates. These are the exact emails that we are using to promote our business, and you can learn from them.

See how we are doing this? Just change the words, make it yours, make it relevant to your course one-pager and make it relevant to your own market research. That's why you needed to do the market research. That's why from the very beginning I said never skip any steps.

Module 7-3

CHAPTER 7 (CONTINUED)

Offer Wrap-Up Page

The offer wrap-up page is a shorter version of a sales page that we usually use at the end of a webinar. The difference between an offer wrap-up page and a sales page is that the sales page usually includes a video were it explains to people why they need to buy the program or the product you're selling. Since people have watched a webinar for 90 minutes, you don't want to give them another 20-, 30- or 40-minute video to watch, so you use the offer wrap-up page.

If you have your course one-pager, you have everything that you need to put together your offer wrap-up page.

At the top of the offer wrap-up page, you have the logo of your course. Then you're going to put the name of the course, and either the subtitle or the promise of the course.

Next, you're going to have a sentence like this: "Yes, [insert your own name], I am ready to invest in myself." Follow this with the benefit of investing in this course.

For example, in my case, the benefit of my program is to change other people's lives and businesses. I make a massive difference in my business by creating and selling profitable online courses. Whatever it is in your words, for whatever you teach, you can replace it here, with the benefits of your course.

You continue with, "I understand that I am getting access to a one-time offer worth...", and then you are going to put a certain amount for the price.

Don't worry about how to price the course because I'm going to explain how to calculate the value of your course in the next chapter.

The sales page continues, "I understand that this offer is available for a limited time, and can be taken down. I also understand as far as the [insert the name of your course], I would get access to...", and here is where you are going to list the features of the course, which you wrote on your course one-pager.

Next, on the offer wrap-up page, you'll have a couple of "Buy Now" or "Get Instant Access Now" buttons. One will be for full payment, and you might have another one for a payment plan depending on the cost of the course. You will connect these to a payment processor.

Finally, you'll need to have the money-back guarantee. On this page, I also have the testimonials of my students, but that section can be easily removed if this is the first time that you are running the course, and you don't have many testimonials.

However, remember, the first time that you were selling your course, you were not selling it by using a webinar, or by selling the landing page; you were selling your course by doing the market research and doing secondary calls.

So, in reality, by the time you are building your webinar funnel, you will probably have testimonials, or you can get them from your beta class.

If you don't have them, that's not a big deal at all; you can simply remove that section from the sales page. End the page with the money-back guarantee.

Module 7-4

CHAPTER 7 (CONTINUED)

How to Calculate the Value of the Course

How should we calculate the value of the course? You calculate every feature or component of the course separately. You ask, "How much is the value of each section of the course on its own if the person doesn't want to get it within my program?" I'll use my own course as an example.

Course content:

The first part of our program is to have instant access to all course material as soon as they register so that they can get started right away. So, what's the value of an entire course, which has 20 hours of content plus lots of PDFs, templates, and everything else?

Usually, that kind of course sells in the market for somewhere between $500 and $2,000. That's the value of the course if they want to buy it somewhere else, so that's what you put as the value of your course.

Now, that is not necessarily the price of your course. That's the value.

Let's say you're giving eight weekly live training sessions. What's the value of doing eight weekly live training sessions with you? I calculate every hour of working with me in a group at $250.

In our program, every class is two hours, so every class is about a $500 value. We have eight weekly classes, so that's a $4,000 value.

Class recordings:

Then you have access to the recordings of the live classes in case you miss them. What's the value of that? If a student just watches the recordings of the live training and doesn't show up live in the classes, that would be about half the value of attending all the classes live, so it's about $2,000. We have a step-by-step weekly plan to create and sell your course profitably with massive success. What's the value of a step-by-step plan? Let's say $500.

Support group membership:

Members get lifetime access to an Ultimate Course Formula support group where they can ask any questions they have, as long as they're building their online courses. That could be valued at $1,000 to $2,000.

By the way, if you're giving a person lifetime access, you want to explain this – that this means they have access as long as your company exists, as long as you're delivering this course, as long as that platform exists. That's written in our student agreement, what "lifetime" means in our case.

You add all this up and let's say the total value of the program works out to $10,000. But, what's the price of the program? $2,000.

What about the exclusive offer that happens in the next three days after the webinar? It can be a 50% discount, a 75% discount, whatever that is.

But, for the value, that's the way you calculate it – you determine the value of each feature separately, and then you add all of them up.

Module 7-5

CHAPTER 7 (CONTINUED)

The Post-Webinar Funnel

The next part of building your webinar funnel is having a great post-webinar follow-up series. The post-webinar follow-up series is made up of the emails you send out to people to remind them that they attended this webinar, they wanted to buy the course, but they haven't bought the course yet.

As I mentioned, there are several samples of these emails that you can get access to when you invest on Ultimate Course Formula Training. Here are five sample emails that I would recommend to you.

The first email provides a link to the recording of the webinar. You want to give that to them right after the webinar.

On Day 2, a second email is sent out that we call the "The Change," which describes the change your course is going to make in their lives. 3-5. Then on the last day – the third day after the webinar – you're going to write three emails: "Deadline tonight," "Worst case scenario," and then "Going…going…gone."

Let's look in more detail at the first email with the recording. The subject line is, "Recording of the [webinar topic] and…"

For example, for my webinar follow-up email, I would put, "Recording of the Online Course Creation Webinar and…" If your topic is weight loss, the subject line would be: "Recording of the Weight Loss Webinar and…" You end the subject line with ellipses to peak the reader's curiosity.

Then, inside the email, you'll write: "Hi [first name], I'm getting so many raving reviews about the webinar we did yesterday on [topic of the webinar]. If you missed it or want to watch it again, you can go to ..." and you give them the webinar replay link.

When you are sending the email we call "The change," in the subject line you would put, "The change that..." and insert the topic.

So, in my case, it's "The change that your online course can make." If you're teaching weight loss, "The change that your weight loss can make." If you're going with stress management, "The change that decreasing your stress can make."

Then in the email, you talk about all the changes your course can make in their life.

Choose five changes to state. As long as you use the words that your customers used answering Question 2 when you did your market research, you are good to go.

Module 7-6

CHAPTER 7 (CONTINUED)

Tools For Your Webinar Funnel

You will need the following tools to build Build Your Webinar Funnel. First, you want to make sure that you sign up for a ClickFunnels account. To do that, use my affiliate link: <u>Successroadacademy. com/clickfunnels</u>

By using ClickFunnels you can build all your funnel pages. If you invest in purchasing Ultimate Course Formula program, you will get access to my funnel pages which you can copy to your system with one click.

By doing so my entire funnel will be copied to your system so that you will have all the different components of the funnel already set up for you. You will have the webinar replay page, the webinar sign-up page, and the offer wrap-up page. You will get everything that you need for your funnel.

You will also need to register for Active Campaign. No other tool like Mailchimp, Aweber, Constant Contact and other tools can do what we want to do in the automated funnel.

You can register for Active Campaign through my affiliate link below: <u>Successroadacademy.com/activecampaign</u>

You will also need Webinar Jam to be able to do the automation part of the webinar follow up series. You can register for Webinar Jam through my affiliate link at: <u>Successroadacademy.com/webinarjam</u>

When you invest on Ultimate Course Formula online program, you will get access to the video training on how to setup the entire technical part of your webinar funnel. It's virtually impossible to include all those technical parts in a book.

CHAPTER 8

Five Types of Promotional Partners

In this chapter, we're going to talk about traffic and how to get joint ventures so they can promote your webinars and your presentations, put you on the stage, etc. Let's start with the five types of joint ventures that are out there and how you can get access to them.

I'm not going to go into too many details on that, because when you come to the event, we'll build the funnel for you, and that's the time that makes more sense to think about joint ventures. However, I want to give you a general idea about how joint ventures and traffic work.

When it comes to joint ventures, there are five types of JVs or promotional partners. So sometimes I use the term joint ventures, and sometimes I say, promotional partners. They mean the same thing, in the general sense.

Sneezers

The first group of promotional partners that can refer clients to you can help you promote your course, are called the "sneezers." What does that mean?

Sneezers are people who know you, like you and trust you. They have used your services before. They know who your best customers are, and any time they see a person who can benefit from your services or products, they spread the word about you. That's why we call them sneezers because they're sneezing about you.

So, who are the sneezers? Generally, people in your family and friends can be great sneezers for you. Also, people with whom you have shared some pieces of content and who really like you.

They connected with your story, and now they can spread the word about you. Also, your current and past clients can be great sneezers for you.

If you have been in the market for some time, you have been teaching people, but you don't have an affiliate program, you don't have a system where people can refer clients to you for your online course, what you can do is invite all your past students to take your online course. You can give them a very deep discount, but you want to help them to take this course so they will become sneezers for you.

Now, you don't have to give them a discount, by the way. They can pay you in full, but every person has a different situation.

In general, you want people who know you and trust you to study your course, so that they can refer you to other clients. So that's the first group – the sneezers.

Favor Motivated

The second group of promotional partners is called the favor- motivated promotional partner. These are the ones who say, "I will promote you if you promote me back."

This works well if you have a mailing list, a podcast, a YouTube show, or a blog that has a good readership. Then you can attract many people who are favor motivated. So you say, "You know what? You have a mailing list of people in my niche market. I will promote you on my podcast, interview you for my YouTube channel, and send some emails to my mailing list for you, and I would like for you to do the same for me. I want you to promote me in return. I'll promote you, so you promote me."

Now there's a key lesson here. If you don't have a podcast, if you don't have a YouTube channel, or you don't have a mailing list, it's a really good time to start one, because then you can unlock a lot of favor-motivated promotional partners for yourself.

Content Motivated

The third type of promotional partner is called the content- motivated promotional partner. These are people who care about your content. For example, think about this. If your target market is moms, or if your target market is entrepreneurs, members of your target market usually belong to a network, an association, or a group.

These groups, associations, and networks they belong to, the magazines they read, podcasts they listen to, and YouTube channels they watch, they all need content.

If you have great content, then you can show up on those podcasts, interview shows, radio series, etc. Or, you can do a presentation for an association or organization. You can share your content, you're going to attract customers, and they're going to buy your course.

I highly recommend that if you don't have a list of the networks, associations, and groups that your target market belongs to, start building a list. That way, you can attract a lot of content-motivated promotional partners.

Success Road Academy has a course called Promotional Partners Master Class that covers all these details, and when you come to the Marketing Mastery Summit event, if you have a VIP ticket, you get the Promotional Partners Master Class as part of your benefits. In that class, you will learn the exact details about what emails to send and how to attract people.

Money Motivated

The fourth group of promotional partners is money-motivated promotional partners. The reason they are promoting you is that they want to get paid. Now, that doesn't mean the sneezers favor- motivated, or content-motivated JV's don't want to be paid but, the money-motivated promotional partner's number 1 value is getting paid. They'll say, "If I promote you, and I send you 100 clicks, will I get $200 back? So will you pay me $2 per click that I send you?"

The entire conversation with them is about money with them. Unfortunately, in the market, the way many people who talk about joint ventures are positioning this is that everybody cares about the money, but that's not the reality.

Yes, people want to get paid for the things that they are doing, but the best promotional partners are those who care about the content match. They care whether the content they are promoting to their mailing list is a good match for their mailing list. And, if it is, they are happy to promote you, as long as you can do a favor for them back, such as promoting them back or providing them with content.

Don't think the only reason people want to promote you is money, but if you go with that mindset to the market, then that's the only type of JV that you are going to find.

Credibility Seekers

The last group of joint ventures you can find are called credibility seekers. These are people who want to promote you because of your credibility. And, the way you build your credibility, as we covered in Chapter 3, is with your marketing.

When you're building your credibility, you are positioning yourself as a credible company. You want people who look at your package, look at your brand, look at the things you are doing and say, "Yes, you know what? This looks like a very credible package. I can put myself on board with this person, and I'd like to promote this person."

Obviously, the bigger your brand becomes, the easier it becomes to get credibility seekers.

If you're starting, I would suggest you start with content-motivated promotional partners and sneezers. Those are the easiest ones to reach out to. Those are the easiest ones to activate. Even to this day, in my business, the content-motivated JVs and the sneezers are the biggest sources of income in my company.

> *Yes, people want to get paid for the things that they are doing, but the best joint ventures are joint ventures that care about the content match.*

In Closing

Over the past few years, I have taught more than a thousand people how to successfully create and launch their online courses, and the biggest mistake I've seen with online course creators is that they don't take action on teaching their *first* course.

The biggest mistake I keep seeing is that people wait until they have their best course.

The problem with waiting to have your best course is that you will never have your best course unless you teach your first course to a group of students. The first course is going to be your best course when you launch it; then you improve on your first course because you never want to have a second course that is worse than your first course.

You can never, ever wait until you have the best course to launch, and as a result of gaining experience from what you teach to the first group of students, you can decide how to improve your course.

Always keep this in mind when you get to Step 4 of *Ultimate Course Formula*, where you have put together your course one-pager. You have to go out there, and you have to sell the course. You remember that the course that you are selling should be a live online training and you can use Zoom to run that course.

What that allows you to do is gain the confidence and the competence to put together your content, and at the same time gives you feedback and allows you to see the results you're making in people's lives.

Never hold back on the information that you have, and never wait until you have the best course. You will gain huge amounts of experience *only* if you teach your course.

The second mistake I've seen course creators make is waiting until they have taught their entire course before starting to improve the course they are teaching. That usually happens when people are teaching their course for the first time live.

After each class, they get the feedback, but they don't change and improve the content that they just taught right away. Instead, they plan to go back later to review the content and improve it.

The problem with that is after a few weeks of teaching your course; you're going to forget about the feedback people gave you. You won't be able to go back and improve your course content the way you could have if you had taken that feedback and implemented it right away.

I highly suggest, even if you want to create a course that you can sell in evergreen mode, meaning that you can sell it indefinitely, you teach your course live first, and right after getting feedback from the first students, edit your course and re-record it right away in the same week.

That allows you to finish your recorded course right after finishing your live course. I have seen this so many times that people don't do this right away and that puts them behind for six months or a year and, as a result, they don't get their course launched in the appropriate time.

The third mistake I have seen with entrepreneurs and with course creators is that they get into this mindset of, "What if people don't want to learn from me and what if they don't want to see my course?" They start comparing themselves with all their competitors.

Let me tell you a secret. Every single coach that creates videos hates their videos. So when you look at your own video, you're not going to fall in love with it, but you're not alone. Almost everyone who creates courses, when they watch their own videos don't see the value and they judge themselves and the content of their course. Remember that it's your target market that matters. They're the ones who need to get value from your course. It's only their opinion that matters.

One of the benefits of teaching your course live is that you can see the impact you can make in people's lives and you can see the changes they are making in their lives or business or environment, and, as a result of that, you will never want to stop teaching. That's the biggest benefit of coaching for you as a coach – to see the change that you're making in the world every single day.

Don't hold back. Follow every step of Ultimate Course Formula. Never skip any steps and complete each step before moving to the next step.

Make sure you find your way to the live event in Vancouver where we can help plan marketing your course and other services through public speaking which is the most important tool that you will use to make money with. You. Can reserve your seat to the event here: MarketingMasterySummit.com/exclusive

I can't wait to see you at the event where we are going to create a step by step plan to market your course.

About Iman Aghay

Iman Aghay is a serial entrepreneur, best-selling author, and international speaker. He founded Success Road Academy in 2010, which is one of the largest Information Marketing Training Centers in the world. He harnesses the power of the Internet and combines it with effective in-person marketing to help business owners grow their companies, and professionals position themselves as the go-to experts in their fields.

Also, he is the creator of "Ultimate Course Formula," which helps experts create and sell online courses with a simple step by step process in 60 days or less.

Iman has worked with over 15,000 business owners in the past few years in his seminars, events, webinars, group coaching, and one on one coaching sessions.

Iman is a TEDx speaker and has spoken on the stage over 400 times in the past few years in front of audiences of thousands of people. He has shared the stage with Gary Vaynerchuk, Dan Martell, Sean Stephenson, Ted McGrath, John Chow as well as presenters from the David Suzuki Foundation, Hootsuite, Yelp and many others.

Iman arrived in Vancouver in 2009 with limited knowledge of English, no network, and no job. After studying the most successful businesses in the world, he created a marketing system that combined the most effective marketing strategies used by those businesses. He started his own company, applied his system and in a very short time:

- Founded Entrepreneurs International Network, which is a group of business networks in 5 countries in the world with over 20,000 members today.

- Founded the largest information marketing training center in Canada, "Success Road Academy" with over 10,000 attendees to its events in the past three years.

- Taught his system and helped thousands of people to build successful businesses for themselves. Today he has clients from Courtney, Canada to Sidney, Australia.

He has been featured on CBC radio, Shaw TV, Fox, CBS News, ABC, NBC and has made the cover of Immigrants Magazine. Iman's passion is helping entrepreneurs to succeed.

He won the People's Choice Award for being one of the top 25 immigrants in Canada and shares this honor with media mogul Peter Legge, Dragon's Den star Robert Herjavec and John Furlong, CEO of Vancouver Organizing Committee for the 2010 Olympic and Paralympic Winter Games.

Made in United States
Orlando, FL
11 April 2024